TRIUMPH AND TRAGEDY IN THE CROWSNEST PASS

THANK YOU FOR ATTENDING
OUR VETERANS' SUPPER
FRIDAY, OCTOBER 14TH, 2005
YOUR BEING HERE MEANS
A LOT.

THANK YOU,
THE ROYAL CANADIAN LEGION
BRANCH #7 BLAIRMORE, ALBERTA

TRIUMPH AND TRAGEDY IN THE CROWSNEST PASS

Edited by Diana Wilson

Heritage
House

Library and Archives Canada Cataloguing in Publication
Triumph and tragedy in the Crowsnest Pass / edited by
Diana Wilson—2nd ed.

ISBN 1-894384-16-4

1. Crowsnest Pass Region (Alta. and B.C.)—History.
2. Disasters—Crowsnest Pass Region (Alta. and B.C.)—History.
I. Wilson, Diana, 1958-

FC3695.C76T73 2005   971.23'4   C2004-900573-1

Cover photo courtesy of the Frank Slide Interpretive Centre, Alberta
Community Development; inset: Provincial Archives of Alberta.

Cover and interior design and layout by Frances Hunter.

Edited by Diana Wilson, Karla Decker, and Art Downs.

This book is set in Adobe Minion, Albertus, and Syntax.

Heritage House acknowledges the financial support for its publishing
program from the Government of Canada through the Book
Publishing Industry Development Program (BPIDP), The Canada
Council for the Arts, and the Province of British Columbia through
the British Columbia Arts Council.

Heritage House Publishing Co. Ltd.
#108-17665 66A Ave.
Surrey, BC, Canada V3S 2A7
greatbooks@heritagehouse.ca
www.heritagehouse.ca

Printed in Canada by Friesens, Altona, Manitoba

The Canada Council | Le Conseil des Arts
for the Arts | du Canada

BRITISH COLUMBIA
ARTS COUNCIL
We acknowledge the support of the Province of British Columbia
through the British Columbia Arts Council

CONTENTS

George Rudeychuk was a coal miner typical of thousands who worked in the Crowsnest Pass in the early 1900s.

ACKNOWLEDGEMENTS

Sincere thanks to the following people for their generous assistance: Bob Harvey, a former B.C. deputy minister of highways and author of books and articles on B.C.'s transportation history, for the use of rare accounts by and about the people of the Crowsnest Pass; Monica Field, manager of the Frank Slide Interpretive Centre, for her invaluable donation of her personal time to do fact-checking, and for providing the cover photo; Don Wilson, author and historian, for his fascinating and well-researched web site about the Crowsnest Highway (please visit this site at http://www.crowsnest-highway.ca); Cindy Gallinger of the Elk Valley Coal Corporation, for providing extensive information on the company's current coal-mining processes; Janna van Kessel, executive director of the Crowsnest Pass Ecomuseum Trust Society, for updating our information on the Bellevue Underground Mine tours and museum; Wendy Zack, operations manager and curator of the Crowsnest Museum for updating our information on new exhibits at the museum; Lori Sugden, map specialist for the map collection at the University of Victoria library, for sourcing period maps; Brian Jeffery, archivist for the Cranbrook Historical Archives at The Canadian Museum of Rail Travel, for sourcing a hard-to-find photo of Colonel James Baker; designer Frances Hunter, for her standard of excellence in layout and design, and for her astute, roving eye; Karla Decker, assistant editor at Heritage House, for her expert copy-editing and assistance with captions; Vivian Sinclair, Heritage House's managing editor, for her endless wealth of advice and support; and, last but not least, Rodger Touchie, publisher at Heritage House, who believes that the history and stories of western Canada are worth remembering.

PREFACE

The origin of the name "Crowsnest Pass" is a topic that sparks hot debate. A common theory maintains that it's a translation of the Cree Indian name, kah-ka-ioo-wut-tshis-tun, and refers simply to the presence of crows and their nests in the trees at the base of Crowsnest Mountain. Native legends provide other, more interesting, explanations. In Blackfoot mythology, the spirit Napi created the world and when he was through, he climbed to the top of Turtle Mountain and vanished, choosing the mountain as his final resting place. One legend handed down relates that Blackfoot Indians ambushed a party of raiding Crow Indians from Montana in 1853 at the base of that mountain. In the midst of the ensuing battle, a huge rock broke away from the mountain, killing about 200 men. The Blackfoot believed that Napi had delivered a warning. They stopped the battle and carved a message into the rock that fell. It read: "Peace forever in this valley. Let no one break the peace."[1] Thinking that the mountain must be moving itself slowly forward, stone by stone, the Blackfoot named it Turtle Mountain. They referred to it as "The Mountain That Walks" and took pains to stay out of its advancing path. The region was named "Crow's Nest Pass" to honour the Crow Indians that died in the battle.

In another version, the Blackfoot managed to trap the marauding Crow Indians and kill them in a "nest" at the base of an unnamed mountain. They named the mountain "Crow's Nest" to commemorate their victory, and the pass took the name of the mountain.

The spelling of "Crowsnest" has also varied over time. It is found in historic records as Crow's Nest, Crows Nest, Crow Nest, and Crowsnest. Local residents favour Crow's Nest. The official spelling—and the one used in this book, except when quoting proper names or the words of others—is Crowsnest.

View of Highway 3, the Crow Route, through the Crowsnest Pass, circa 1960.

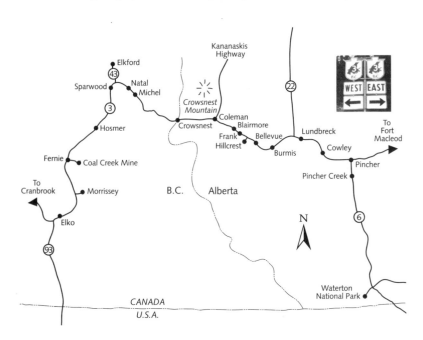

The Crowsnest Pass is about 60 miles long, straddling the southern provincial border in the Canadian Rockies from Lundbreck on the Alberta side to Elko in British Columbia.

Pass of Triumph, Pass of Tragedy

The Crowsnest Pass region is a storied land of treasure and disaster, with topography as stunning and diverse as any to be found in Canada. It encompasses an array of postcard views from sleepy river valleys, forested foothills, and grassy ridges to craggy, volcanic mountains, scree slopes, and high alpine meadows where mountain goats, elk, and bighorn sheep graze among wisps of cloud. The Crowsnest Highway—Highway 3, or The Crow Route—bears travellers from Hope, B.C., through the Crowsnest Pass and on to Medicine Hat, Alberta, a journey of about 700 miles. The pass itself is about 60 miles long, straddling the southern provincial border in the Canadian Rockies from Lundbreck on the Alberta side to Elko in British Columbia. A tunnel of perpetual winds that often exceed 60 miles an hour, the pass marks a natural division between Kananaskis Country to the north and Waterton Lakes Provincial Park to the south.

Perhaps nowhere else in Canada has tragedy struck so often in so small an area. In disasters ranging from avalanches and town-consuming fires to rock slides and mine explosions, more than 600 men, women, and children have been burned alive, crushed by boulders, or blown apart. The endurance shown by residents of the region—the determination to pick up the pieces and rebuild time after time—is testimony to the triumph of the human spirit in the face of hardship.

This land of the Crowsnest calls out its challenge and the people respond. Not surprisingly, the Crowsnest Pass is home to one of the most incredible and historic achievements in human perseverance and ingenuity: a railway rammed through the pass in only 18 months, using tools and technology since relegated to museums.

The story of the triumphs and tragedies of the Crowsnest Pass is bound up with the story of coal. Coal mining was the driving force behind the building of the railroad. Steam locomotives needed coal to run, and coal needed locomotives to get to industrial markets. And coal mines account for the worst disasters. In the miles of underground tunnels, over 500 men have died over the years in searing explosions of coal dust, or from invisible clouds of deadly vapour known as "afterdamp."

The Frank Slide killed at least 81 people when 90 million tons of limestone fell from Turtle Mountain in just 90 seconds, burying the mine works, homes, and businesses nestled at the mountain's foot.

Turtle Mountain's geological structure is notoriously unstable, and the final trigger for the catastrophe has been attributed to a plunge in temperature that froze water trapped in giant cracks in the rock. Expanding ice jettisoned the mountain's face. But the coal mine was named a contributing factor: some say the miners delved too deep too fast, disturbing the roots of the restless Mountain That Walks.

In the local folklore, even the Fernie fire that razed the entire town in 1908 is linked to coal. Legend has it that William Fernie, a prominent early settler active in developing the coalfields, brought a curse of "death, fire, hunger, and all human miseries"[2] down on the Elk Valley when he jilted a Ktunaxa chief's daughter for love of the "black diamond."

Coal in the region was well known but little valued by the successive early cultures whose presence in the Crowsnest Pass is documented from 8,000 years ago. Father Jean de Smet, a missionary who worked with the Ktunaxa (or Kootenay) Indians in what is today southern British Columbia and northern Montana, was the first to note the

Miners and their horses at Hillcrest. Coal mines in the Crowsnest Pass region have claimed over 500 lives.

economic potential of coal on the Elk River. In 1845, he wrote in a letter that he had seen large pieces of coal along the river, declaring: "I am convinced that this fossil could be abundantly procured."[3] His words were prophetic, as the region would prove to contain some of the world's largest coal reserves.

Twenty-eight years later, Michael Phillipps and John Collins were prospecting for gold but found only coal when they became the first non-native people known to have traversed the Crowsnest Pass. History records little of Collins, crediting the event to Phillipps, an Englishman who arrived in 1864 to clerk for the Hudson's Bay Company. In 1870, he left the firm and started a ranch and sawmill near present-day Roosville, B.C. At the same time, he trapped and prospected, following to their headwaters many tributaries of the area's two main rivers, the Elk and the Flathead. On that fateful expedition in 1873, Phillipps, Collins, and four packhorses left on a prospecting and trapping trip up the Elk River. As Phillipps later wrote in his account of the journey "… formation of the country was promising for coal but very discouraging for the gold hunter." After they reached Michel Creek (named after Chief Michel of the upper Ktunaxa), they followed it eastward. They were astonished to find large trails not made by elk, the main wildlife in the region. Then they noticed that the trees were covered with buffalo hair, but buffalo did not inhabit the western side of the mountains. Phillipps wrote, "It was evident to both of us that we had passed through the Rocky Mountains without going over any range. This is the first trip ever made by what is now known as the Crow's Nest Pass."[4]

The following year, Phillipps and three companions returned to the Elk River area to explore further. They branched off up a creek they named Morrissey, after Jim Morrissey, "the real old miner"[5] of the group. Still there was only coal and no traces of gold. On the next creek, coal was even more abundant. They named it Coal Creek, for as Phillipps noted: "We could find nothing but coal and coal everywhere."[6] Despite his disappointment, Phillipps collected coal samples and sent them off to Dr. George W. Dawson, director of the Geological Survey of Canada, little knowing what forces of change he had set in motion.

Phillipps still had faith in the potential of the Crowsnest country. Of the route he and trapper John Collins had discovered through the Rockies, he wrote: "I saw the advantage of a pass through a great rocky range without a mountain to go over and I determined to work for a trail."[7]

British Columbia's government representative in the area, Gold Commissioner William Fernie (of the Elk Valley curse), proved a formidable obstacle. "The Indians say there is no Pass," he stated, "and there is no use spending money to make a trail [to] nowhere."[8]

Undaunted, Phillipps cut a rough trail through the pass with the help of some friends. In 1874, Robert Galbraith, MLA for the Kootenay district, secured funding for Phillipps to improve the trail. The Galbraith family owned and operated a ferry service on the Kootenay River and would profit from increased traffic through the region.

Phillipps worked at improving and extending the trail for several years, at one point hiring William Fernie's brother, Peter. Peter Fernie had worked in the coal industry, and Phillipps was eager to get his opinion on the quality of the coal. When Phillipps showed him the coal along the trail, Fernie was not encouraging, saying, "If that's your coal, I don't think much of it."[9] Peter Fernie would later become

Left: *History credits Michael Phillipps, an early settler and prospector, with the discovery of the Crowsnest Pass.*

Right: *Brothers William and Peter Fernie were skeptical about the potential for development in the Crowsnest Pass. They later became partners in the first coal company in the region.*

a partner with brother William in the first coal company in the Elk Valley, although, as Phillipps later wrote with a hint of bitterness, "William Fernie had nothing to do with the discovery of coal in the Elk Valley."[10]

❖   ❖   ❖

In 1879, the trail through the Crowsnest Pass was completed. Two years later, the Canadian Pacific Railway (CPR) explored the area as a possible route for its transcontinental line. But the Canadian government opposed the route for military reasons, considering it too close to the U.S. border. Rogers Pass to the north subsequently became the Rocky Mountain crossing for Canada's first coast-to-coast rail link.

Meanwhile, Dr. Dawson of the Geological Survey had been so impressed with the coal sample Phillipps sent him that he visited the Crowsnest region several times to assess its potential. In 1882, Dawson published a report proclaiming that the area "was destined to be one of the most valuable and most productive coalfields in Canada."[11] Apart from heating the homes of a few isolated settlers, however, the coal would have no commercial value until there was a viable means of getting it to market.

A champion was needed, someone with unshakeable faith in both the value of the coal and the necessity of a railway through the Crowsnest Pass, someone with the drive and ambition to accomplish great things at any cost. In 1884, that champion arrived in the person of Colonel James Baker.

Baker was born in London, England, on January 6, 1830. Educated by a private tutor, he went on to earn a Master of Arts degree at Cambridge. Baker married Sarah Louise White and fathered a son, Valentine Hyde Baker. With the Indian Navy, Baker surveyed the Arabian coast and helped stamp out the slave trade in that region. Later he fought with the British Army in the Crimean War, attaining the rank of lieutenant colonel. After retiring from the army, Baker travelled for several years, and was later a private secretary to the Duke of Westminster, one of the most important landlords in London.

His brothers, Sir Samuel Baker and Valentine Aker Pasha Baker, both famous explorers and writers, had already assured themselves of a place in British history books and James Baker, eager to distinguish himself as a man of consequence as well, was determined to see

Colonel James Baker lobbied 10 years for a railroad through the Crowsnest Pass. Development of the coalfields followed rapidly on the heels of the railroad.

his name written in the annals of the New World. It became his life's mission to have a railroad built through the Crowsnest Pass—and into the coalfields.

Following on the heels of the railway, major companies began developing the massive coal outcroppings that flanked the pass for some 45 miles of its 60-mile length. One gigantic seam in British Columbia was found to be 180 feet thick—in some places, 600 or more. In addition to being plentiful, the coal proved excellent for converting to coke, which was used to power the railway engines.

Mines developed rapidly, and communities sprang up to serve them. William Fernie handpicked a crew of Cape Breton miners and constructed his mine site at Coal Creek. Mines also appeared at Natal, Michel, Morrissey, and Hosmer. On the Alberta side, seven years before that territory would officially be a province of Canada, Blairmore was the first coal-mining community, born in 1898. Soon there were 10 communities within 14 miles, with producing mines at Passburg, Bellevue, Hillcrest, Frank, Lille, Blairmore, and Coleman.

While the millions of tons of coal pouring from the mine tipples created prosperity, extracting it resulted in dreadful disasters that touched virtually every community with terrible fingers. In most of the mines flanking the pass, the coal contained large quantities of methane and other trace gases that, when mixed with air, created a volatile condition known as "firedamp." The mining methods also created clouds of highly explosive coal dust. Combined, the coal dust and firedamp were deadly: a methane gas fire usually resulted in a cataclysmic coal-dust explosion.

Even more dangerous than an explosion was "afterdamp"—a deadly mixture of gases, mostly carbon monoxide, left after an explosion had burned oxygen from the air. Scores of miners who survived devastating underground blasts were killed by the afterdamp. Death in the mines became so common that for nearly 50 years the federal department of mines and minerals issued statistics showing the number of tons of coal mined per serious injury and fatality.

Fernie, however, has had tragedies beyond its mine disasters. The fire of 1904 wiped out the community's entire business section; thankfully, no lives were lost. But the fire of 1908 destroyed everything except for a small group of buildings separated from the main town by lawns. Ten people in the community of 6,000 died, and losses amounted to a then-astronomical $5 million.

In all, more than 600 people have died in various tragedies in the Crowsnest Pass region. On the following pages are accounts of the three worst, which shattered the communities of Frank, Hillcrest, and Fernie.

But first came the railroad.

The Frank Slide dominates the eastern end of the Alberta section of the Crowsnest Pass.

RAILROAD THROUGH THE CROWSNEST

Diana Wilson

By 1886, the idea of building a railroad was not yet a glimmer in Colonel James Baker's mind, but the forces of destiny were already moving through him as his fingers closed around the deed to his new estate. Baker may have felt a thrill of apprehension bracing him for what was to come as his eyes swept appraisingly over the 18,000 acres of flat, mixed forest and fertile meadows where he hoped to build a town. Proud to be making his mark in the Kootenay district after only one year, Baker might have let his gaze linger on the eastern horizon, toward the Rocky Mountains fanning misty blue and rose-tinted under a clear morning sky, and to England beyond, where his family would be waiting for news of his accomplishments in the New World. He named his estate Cranbrook, after his ancestral home in Kent.

Baker hired local surveyor Fred Aylmer to stake out lots, then prepared for the new citizens of Cranbrook by stocking his general store with all the accoutrements of refinement and necessity. Irish linen and English bone china were soon rubbing shoulders with sturdy axes and iron nails on the shelves. But Galbraith's Ferry 10 miles to the northeast, a ferry service across the Kootenay River established during the Wild Horse Creek gold rush of 1864, was on the steamship route and diverted traffic away from the upstart Cranbrook.

Not given to despair, Baker cast about for other opportunities. When he came across a report by Dr. George Dawson of the Geological Survey about massive coal deposits in the Crowsnest Pass region, Baker quickly formed a syndicate with Alymer and William and Peter Fernie to assess the coal measures.

The Fernie brothers, Scottish immigrants who had been in the Kootenays for over 20 years, were familiar with the Crowsnest Pass. William had opposed Michael Phillipps' project to build the first trail through the pass because the Indians had told him it did not exist. Peter later worked with Phillipps on clearing that very trail and building two bridges. He had seen the coal, but had dismissed its value after a cursory examination.

While Baker entered the race for one of two Kootenay district seats in the provincial legislature, a position that would aid him in his business pursuits, Peter and William went into the pass for a closer look at the coal. As they explored, the brothers realized the extent of the coalfields, which would prove to be the largest in Canada. Greatly excited, they returned to report their findings to the syndicate.

Baker, by this time a newly elected MLA, was eager to begin developing the coalfields. But before his syndicate could act, a problem arose that would divert his attention for many months.

It began when Baker decided to raise cattle on the meadow beside his store. This meadow, part of Baker's estate, was also hereditary Ktunaxa grazing land, known as Joseph's Prairie. Chief Joseph, for whom the meadow was named, had had an understanding with the former owner of the property, John Galbraith (of Galbraith's Ferry), stipulating that the Ktunaxa could forever graze stock on Joseph's Prairie. Joseph's successor, Chief Isidore, was outraged when Baker fenced the meadow.

Isidore spurred his horse toward Galbraith's Ferry, and the community held an emergency meeting to hear the distraught chief's grievance. John Galbraith had passed away, and his younger brother, Robert, could not recall any mention of such an agreement with the Ktunaxa. Although the townspeople sympathized with Isidore, there was nothing they could do; Baker legally owned the meadow.

That winter, tension mounted between the Ktunaxa and the white population. Greatly outnumbered, white settlers began to fear for their safety, since only one policeman looked after the entire southwest corner of B.C. Baker wrote to Ottawa for help. In January 1887, Assistant

Commissioner Colonel Lawrence W. Herchmer of the North West Mounted Police (NWMP) was sent from Victoria to assess the situation. Herchmer sensed trouble brewing, and he recommended that Ottawa send aid to the volatile region. Ottawa dispatched NWMP Major Samuel Benfield Steele from Fort Macleod with his "D" Division, 75 strong.

Before Steele's troop could arrive, the brew erupted. In March, carrying warrants from justices of the peace William Fernie and Michael Phillipps, provincial constable Harry Anderson rode to Isidore's camp with six men and arrested a young Native man, Kapla, for the murder of two American prospectors a few

Chief Isidore of the Ktunaxa clashed with Colonel James Baker in a land dispute over Cranbrook.

years earlier. Constable Anderson put the prisoner in a rickety jailhouse at Wild Horse Creek near Galbraith's Ferry, intent on holding him until the circuit judge arrived.

Infuriated, Isidore armed 25 men from his band and rode to the jailhouse. He demanded the release of Kapla, stating that no white man had ever been held for the murder of an Indian. Anderson barred the jailhouse door, but the Ktunaxa broke it down. Much shaken, Anderson unlocked the cell and freed Kapla. Isidore took the prisoner back to his camp and began working on a plan to expel all white settlers from the area.

Baker renewed his appeal for protection, travelling with Robert Galbraith to Golden to send an urgent telegram to Ottawa. In June, the B.C. branch of Indian Affairs sent Indian Superintendent Dr. Israel Wood Powell to the Kootenay district. Isidore told Powell of his band's struggle for survival. The 49th parallel had divided their traditional hunting grounds in half, and settlers had appropriated the remainder of their land. The Dominion government had granted the Ktunaxa a reserve and advised them to raise cattle, but there was not enough grazing land. Powell wrote a letter to Ottawa recommending that more ranch land be given to Isidore, "even if it mean[t] buying a ranch from a White settler."[12]

In late July, Sam Steele marched into Galbraith's Ferry, carrying orders to quell an Indian uprising. He put his men to work raising a barracks, the first NWMP post to be established west of the Rocky Mountains. Steele called a meeting with Isidore and persuaded the chief to return Kapla for trial at the appointed time, promising fair treatment. Two days before the trial, Ottawa awarded more reserve land to Isidore's band—a 680-acre ranch with excellent winter range at Mayook, beside the Kootenay River. Baker had applied for that property to become part of his proposed 32,000-acre Cranbrook estate, but his application had been turned down.

On September 5, Steele convened court at Galbraith's Ferry to try Kapla for murder. In his memoirs, Steele would later write: "There was no evidence to prove him guilty. [Kapla] showed great intelligence, and it's clear he knew nothing of the murder, which was probably committed by some loose character frequenting the trails."[13] Kapla was released and given provisions for his trip home. After further investigation, some trouble-making white men were punished and the matter was settled.

The problem of Joseph's Prairie remained. Superintendent Powell noted: "It is doubtful if ... this particular piece, first occupied for many years by Joseph and then by Isidore, could, legally, have been purchased by Mr. Galbraith. But it is not desirable that it should be an Indian reserve, as it is a small piece of land in the middle of Colonel Baker's ranch ... and it would always be a source of serious trouble."[14] Steele was ordered to make the Ktunaxa stay off Joseph's Prairie.

Steele wrote to Powell, arguing: "By all the laws of right and wrong the place belongs to Isidore and for me to tell him that his place belongs to another was for me most unpleasant."[15] Powell intervened, reminding Isidore that he now had the winter ranch at Mayook, and that Baker was to pay Isidore for certain improvements on that land.

Isidore chose to bend with the wind, conceding Joseph's Prairie. In a humble speech, he thanked the superintendent for his mercy and for the new grazing lands. Before Powell left, he appointed Michael

Phillipps as the new local Indian agent. Isidore and his band bothered Baker no more.

Peace restored, Steele and his men departed. Robert Galbraith expressed the gratitude felt by the whole town when he proposed a new name for Galbraith's Ferry. Henceforth, the town would be known as Fort Steele, commemorating Sam Steele's efforts to avert an Indian uprising.

❖   ❖   ❖

In the autumn of 1887, with the land dispute settled, Baker turned his attention back to developing the region. Baker's syndicate, now including Baker's son, Hyde, and other individuals, applied for a group

NWMP Major Sam Steele's successful bid to avert an Indian uprising was commended in the renaming of Galbraith's Ferry to Fort Steele.

permit to prospect for coal. They began to acquire large tracts of coal land. It was soon apparent that getting coal was easy, but getting rid of it was not. The Crowsnest trail was little more than a pack route, not wide enough for wagons. They had to find a way to move large quantities of coal to industrial markets.

A vision began to take shape in Baker's mind. What if a railroad were to come right up to their doorstep, buying coal to feed its engines and carrying the surplus to market? Baker's sharp mind darted further. If a railway ran through his land, it would increase its value, diverting traffic from bustling Fort Steele. And if a major station were to be built at Cranbrook, so much the better.

A railroad through the Crowsnest Pass was not so far-fetched. CPR engineers had recommended the route as the easiest way through the Rocky Mountains for the Dominion's cross-continental railroad, but the government had decided against building the national railroad so close to the Americans. Now that the main line was completed through Rogers Pass, far to the north, the proximity of a secondary line farther south was no grave concern because it was not the national line. Baker wangled an introduction to CPR Director George Stephen from Prime Minister Sir John A. Macdonald. Stephen heard Baker out, then reported back to the prime minister: "I have seen Colonel Baker and convinced him that his coal mine is beyond the reach of the CPR. If the coal be all that he thinks it is he ought to be able to sell it to some of the great mining companies in Montana."[16]

Baker went home with a different idea. "Why not build our own railroad?" he urged his syndicate. The B.C. government, keen to open up the west, granted Baker's syndicate a railroad charter in 1888, and lands to lay track.

Elated, Baker and William Fernie formed the Crow's Nest and Kootenay Lake Railway Company. Then the Fernie brothers and Baker formed the first coal company in the Elk Valley, the Crow's Nest Coal and Mineral Company. In 1889, Baker used his legislative assembly position to grant their coal company 10,209 additional acres to prospect for coal. With this sudden rise in his fortunes, Peter Fernie took the opportunity to unload his holdings and retire to Victoria society.

Baker was on a roll, but he had not forgotten his plan to build a town. He formed the Cranbrook and Fort Steele Estates and Townsite Company, yet still no one would buy his Cranbrook lots, so Baker sold them to his own company. Robert Galbraith sold most of Fort Steele as well, and bought stock in the townsite company. His actions sealed the ruin of Fort Steele, because Baker's townsite company had an agreement with Baker's railway company to build a railroad station at Cranbrook. Some say Robert Galbraith didn't know Baker's plan and the disastrous effect it would have on Fort Steele. Others say not only did he know, he colluded.

Baker now possessed land, coal, political power, and a railroad charter. The only thing that he lacked was money. He scoured major cities for investors, without success. In desperation, Baker, now chairman of the standing committee on railroads, offered to help D.C. Corbin, an American railway entrepreneur, penetrate southeastern B.C. to access its resources. Baker had his charter amended to include Corbin, envisioning a railway from the Crowsnest Pass across the bottom of the province to the coast. They called their joint project the British Columbia Southern Railway. (In 1891, the Crow's Nest and Kootenay Lake Railway officially became the British Columbia Southern Railway.) But other members of the standing committee voted against American involvement, and the deal with Corbin fell through.

Baker then courted James J. Hill, a Canadian-born railway magnate who had pushed his Great Northern Railway from his base in St. Paul, Minnesota, across the northern U.S. to the Pacific coast. Hill hated the CPR. He hated even more its general manager, William Cornelius Van Horne, an American railway construction manager who had been with the CPR since 1882. Years earlier, Hill had been the CPR's founding director who had recommended Van Horne for the position of general manager, expressing great enthusiasm for his abilities. But then they argued over the route the CPR should take. Hill wanted it to dip into the U.S. to avoid the Canadian Shield, conveniently linking with his own Great Northern. Van Horne promoted an all-Canadian route. When Van Horne's route won, Hill swore revenge: "I'll get even with him if I have to go to hell for it and shovel coal!"[17] Baker bombarded Hill with offers to build a line under the B.C. Southern charter, but Hill was too busy spitting in Van Horne's face by facilitating the flow of Oriental goods from the Pacific Rim to the eastern states via his Great Northern.

Baker's vast coalfields slumbered undisturbed while flashier discoveries of silver, lead, copper, and zinc seduced a stampede of U.S.

Railway builders William Van Horne (top) and James Hill butted heads over proposed routes for the CPR.

promoters and prospectors into the Kootenays. Van Horne caught the fever, but he did not want to spend money on a major rail line to get at the treasure. In 1892 he devised a complicated rail-and-water route to ship booty north to the CPR main line.

That same year, Corbin pushed a feeder line up into Nelson, becoming the first American railroad to infiltrate the Kootenays. Van Horne's route, with its costly loading and unloading from railcar to barge to railcar, could not compete. There was a public outcry as Corbin gained control of major mining camps and Canadian ore flowed south to connect with Hill's Great Northern, which carried it to smelters at Tacoma, Washington. Van Horne chafed against the American intrusion, and when Prime Minister Macdonald urged him to build Baker's B.C. Southern through the Crowsnest Pass, he gave in. Some general surveying and initial grading between Lethbridge and the Crowsnest was carried out in preparation for a railroad, and it seemed to Baker that his dream was about to be realized.

Then, tragedy struck. Sir John A. Macdonald died, federal financing screeched to a halt, and the curtain came down on Baker's dream. The Conservative government would waffle without strong leadership for the next five years, while the Liberal star on the other end of the political teeter-totter began to rise.

With federal support lost, Baker had to raise capital. His syndicate sold one-third of the Crow's Nest Coal and Mineral Company to a consortium of eastern investors that included the Galt family, owners of the Alberta Railway and Coal Company charter for building a railway through the Crowsnest Pass from the Alberta side. That same year, Baker attained real power with a cabinet appointment as provincial secretary and minister of education, immigration, and mines.

Like an ugly cousin, the coal lay untouched in the Crowsnest Pass while mines bloomed all around it in the Kootenays. Throughout the early 1890s, massive silver, copper, and silver-lead ore deposits were developed. These riches finally attracted Hill's eye, and he began floating ores south on Columbia River barges to his Great Northern Railway. Hill's water route was more successful than Van Horne's, and it was only a matter of time before he would decide to send a feeder rail up into the Kootenays, just as Corbin had done. Baker's syndicate reorganized its coal company to include some Victoria investors, and renamed it the B.C. Coal, Petroleum and Mineral Company; but development still depended on a rail line into their coalfields.

The commencement date on Baker's railway charter came and went. The B.C. government extended the date and granted a whopping 20,000 acres of coal-rich land per mile of track laid, handing over the coveted mineral rights. The syndicate now owned 250,000 acres of coal land. With this attractive package, Baker convinced Van Horne of the coal's worth. At last Baker was able to report to his syndicate that the CPR was committed to the project.

Van Horne leased the Galt family's Alberta line between Lethbridge and Medicine Hat, which would provide a link-up point with Baker's B.C. Southern charter and its huge land grant for construction through the Crowsnest Pass. He began seriously pressing Ottawa for approval to lay steel. The Conservative government remained impotent, so Van Horne surveyed the pass without approval.

Two years passed. Hill was laying track in the Kootenays, pushing his new feeder line, the Kaslo & Slocan Railway, west from Kaslo along the Valley of the Ghosts. Rumour of the vast, untouched coalfields in the Crowsnest Pass was on the wind. Van Horne remarked bitterly: "As soon as there is something like a government to deal with, we will press as vigorously as possible."[18] William Fernie grew tired of waiting and sold his coal shares to federal senators George Cox and Robert Jaffray, owners of an influential Liberal partisan Toronto newspaper, the *Globe*.

In July 1896 Baker got his lucky break. Wilfred Laurier brought the Liberals into power, and the new prime minister fully supported a railway through the Crowsnest Pass. His only question was, who should build it? The CPR was out of public favour for its alleged monopoly and high freight rates. Cox and Jaffray, eager for their shares in Baker's coal company to skyrocket, offered to build the railroad, but Laurier just smiled and shook his head at their lack of experience with large projects.

Baker used his political influence to sway first the B.C. cabinet, then Premier John Turner, to support the CPR. He and Turner wired Laurier in August, imploring the prime minister to strike a deal with the CPR and save Kootenay wealth from the Americans. Van Horne himself appealed to Laurier, stressing for the first time the excellent coal to be had in the east Kootenays. But 1896 drew to a close, and still Laurier hesitated.

Van Horne grew impatient. Hill's railroad was advancing into the Kootenays, and Corbin's control of major mining camps was becoming more entrenched. Van Horne knew it was only a matter of time before Laurier agreed to let the CPR lay the Crowsnest track, but he refused to stand idle while Corbin and Hill picked the Kootenays clean. Van Horne was determined to see a railroad through the pass by the end of 1898, if it took an army. He began preparing to lay steel from Lethbridge to Kuskanook on the east shore of Kootenay Lake.

There was one railroad man who could mobilize a construction army in short order and keep costs reasonable. Michael J. Haney, nicknamed the "Irish Prince" for his commanding presence, had a reputation as a rough and ready, results-oriented organizer of men. He took pride in meeting impossible deadlines with tight budgets, and had recently worked miracles on the Fraser Canyon railway, completing incredible feats of railroad engineering in record time. Van Horne could not have chosen a more efficient construction manager for the Crowsnest project. Haney demanded full control of labour, costs, and materials, and Van Horne, already plagued by politicians wanting jobs and contracts for friends, was relieved to refer them to the scrupulous Haney. He gave Haney carte blanche, as long the railway was completed by November 1898.

Van Horne hired Scottish-born Hugh Lumsden, a capable civil engineer with 29 years' experience locating railway lines in Canada, as chief engineer. Lumsden immediately put his surveyors to work determining the route of the permanent line for the railway to the eastern entrance of the Crowsnest Pass, calculating rock cuts, tunnels, bridge spans, and other such features. They would have to wait until the snow melted to continue the survey through the west side of the pass to Kootenay Lake.

While Van Horne was organizing his team, the political debate raged on. Cox and Jaffray's *Globe*, which had throughout the 1880s vehemently opposed the monopoly of the CPR and denounced the railroad company as "the Tory government on wheels,"[19] now came out in firm support of the CPR's building the Crowsnest line. Opposition papers seized on the about-face. In March 1897, journalists discovered that Cox and Jaffray had purchased a substantial interest in Baker's coal company and stood to benefit from a railway through the region. The *Victoria Daily Times* observed: "Quite a furious controversy is raging among the Toronto papers over who should construct the Crow's Nest Pass Railway."[20]

Michael Haney, hired by the CPR as construction manager on the Crow's Nest Pass Railroad, had a reputation for being difficult.

A few weeks later, a B.C. Liberal MP denounced the "stupendous gall and insatiable greed"[21] of the CPR for seeking government assistance. He also condemned the way public lands were being handed out to companies with railway charters, especially the B.C. Southern. The minister of railways told the Commons he regretted the way the B.C. government allowed valuable coal lands of the Crowsnest Pass to end up in the hands of one company. Baker's name was not mentioned directly.

Laurier may have been holding out for another contender to emerge and save him from an unpopular decision, but no one appeared, and Van Horne felt the hand of fate swing toward the CPR. Although an agreement would not be signed for some months, Van Horne got the nod to start building a railroad.

It would be a race with time. Haney had to lay 330 miles of track in only 18 months. He decided to begin construction at five points simultaneously—Lethbridge, Fort Macleod, Elko, Wardner, and Kootenay Lake. An ingenious problem-solver, Haney had already perfected a method of making prefabricated trestles. The wood could be cut according to the surveyors' calculations and test-assembled in a convenient location. Then the entire structure could be dismantled, transported, and swiftly reassembled on site. All Haney had to do was round up his railway navvies and get started.

The coolies, as Chinese railway labourers were called in the early days of railway construction, were exceptional navvies. On the Fraser Canyon job, Haney had admired their stamina. They endured frontier living without protest, cooked for themselves, drank only boiled water in the form of tea—thus thwarting sickness and disease—and they didn't squander their pay on spirits. But Laurier, responding to popular attitudes of the time, viewed his first major project as an opportunity to test his proposed Alien Labour Law. Haney was informed he could use only Canadian citizens or British citizens expressing a desire to settle in Canada, but no foreign labour. The department of immigration already had 1,000 Welsh farmers lined up for the Crowsnest Pass job.

While Haney found contractors and arranged a recruiting drive for labourers, Laurier pondered how best to appease public concerns about the CPR. He drafted the Crow's Nest Pass Agreement, which allowed the CPR to use Baker's B.C. Southern to construct a branch from

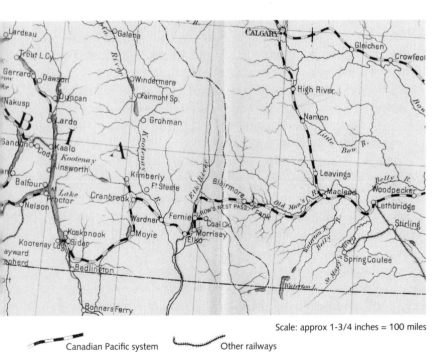

Scale: approx 1-3/4 inches = 100 miles

Canadian Pacific system   Other railways

This 1904 map shows the completed railway through the Crowsnest. Michael Haney began construction at five points simultaneously—Lethbridge, Fort Macleod, Elko, Wardner, and Kootenay Lake.

its main line near Medicine Hat in the Territory of Alberta through the Crowsnest Pass to Kootenay Lake in British Columbia. But the CPR would be regulated by government controls, such as reduced freight rates and a guarantee that competition from other railways would be permitted. Satisfied that the railroad was about to materialize, Baker sold his B.C. Southern stock to the CPR and sat back to await his first glimpse of steel rail glinting under a Cranbrook sun.

By the first week of July 1897, the snow had melted enough that Lumsden could send surveyors into the pass. The Dominion buzzed with the news that construction of the railroad was imminent. Although officially it was still the British Columbia Southern Railway, as Baker had named it, the railroad became commonly referred to as the Crow's Nest Pass Railway. The small local population was not wanting for work, so Haney's hiring agents targeted crowded eastern Canadian cities, where work was scarce.

Another kind of buzz had reached the east as well: *Gold in the Klondike!* Many who were unfit for physical labour—lawyers, actors, barbers, clerks, and cooks—signed on with the CPR to get a free trip west to the gold, planning to escape to the Klondike at the earliest opportunity. Agents promised that the CPR would absorb all travel expenses.

That same month, cabinet passed an Order-in-Council expressly prohibiting the CPR from contracting or subcontracting the construction of the Crow's Nest Pass Railway to any foreigner, or any corporation composed of foreigners. As Haney had been told, the CPR was also forbidden to employ anyone who was not a British subject, a resident of Canada, or an immigrant intending to settle in Canada. From coast to coast, hopes were high that the government was watching out for the interests of Canadian labour.

Dusty and snake-infested, the old NWMP base, Fort Macleod, was chosen as construction headquarters and began to fill up with every variety of stranger. The NWMP kept order, and despite the sudden influx and commotion, there was little lawlessness. The *Macleod Gazette* noted of the newcomers: "They haven't the appearance of men overburdened with this world's wealth, but they all possess good honest faces."[22] Sam Steele was in charge of the post. He was impressed by the speed with which the contractors, under Haney's direction, moved men and materials into the country. During the month of July about 5,000 men and 1,000 teams of horses were employed. Haney paid

Graders prepared the railbed by hand or with the help of horses.

labourers $1.50 per day, and charged them $4 per week for board. In the east Kootenays of 1897, the air was alive with pioneer spirit and there was work for all. Baker's railway dream became a reality on July 14, with an official sod-turning ceremony at Lethbridge. That same day, construction began.

Contractors started a tote road west from the summit of Crowsnest Pass, and east from Kuskanook toward the summit. Along this road would be conveyed tons of supplies for human and beast, construction equipment, tools, blasting powder, horses, mules, and men. Behind the road builders came the railway-clearing and grading gangs, working in sections from one to ten miles in length to take out trees and brush along the right of way and prepare the roadbed to grade specifications set by Lumsden's surveyors. Nearly every mile was virgin country, heavily treed.

Much of the route required cutting heavy rock and tunnels. The hard-rock drillers were a tough, nervy lot with their heavy hand drills. There was always wind, and when it was gusty they were in constant danger of a mis-stroke, injuring or killing the drill holder. The hills rang with the shock of blasting, the thunk of axes, and the crash of falling trees.

One group of French Canadians, expert axe men from the east, had wanted honest work with the railroad, but had been unable to understand the contract. They had signed on, trusting the hiring agent's assurances. Given picks and shovels and placed with a grading gang

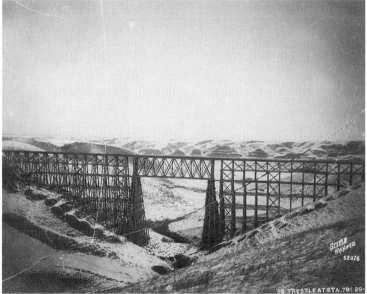

Top: *Tie and steel layers placed the ties and spiked down steel with the rhythm of a percussion band.*

Bottom: *Bridge- and trestle-building gangs spanned the many rivers, creeks, and ravines with prefabricated trestles built in Haneyville, on the outskirts of Fort Macleod.*

The hard-rock drillers were in constant danger of a mis-stroke, injuring or even killing the drill holder.

preparing the roadbed by hand, they dug and levelled, filling wheelbarrow after wheelbarrow with rock and earth. They gestured toward the trees where axes were flying through living timber, but could not make themselves understood by the section boss. Twelve hours a day or more they toiled, taking dirt from one spot and moving it to another, assisted by horses pulling scrapers. They received little sympathy from fellow labourers, who were nursing their own hurts—the soft Welsh farmers with blistered hands, and those others from the east who realized too late that the Klondike was a thousand miles beyond the Crowsnest Pass, and beyond their reach.

The CPR bridge- and trestle-building gangs came along with the graders, ready to span the many rivers, creeks, and ravines using prefabricated trestles brought by wagon and later by rail from Haneyville, the trestle-building site on the outskirts of Fort Macleod. They were well paid at $2.75 for a 10-hour day, with double pay for working overtime on Sundays.

CPR tie and steel layers came next, placing ties and spiking down steel with the rhythm of a percussion band. Last came the CPR ballasters to level the rails and place the finishing touches of unscreened sand and gravel around the ties to set them firmly in place. Hundreds heeded the call to establish a supply line for this railroad army. Teams and wagons took to the make-do roads, hauling hay and oats, camp supplies, and powder for contractors. Supplies on the west side of the pass came north from Jennings, Montana, or Bonner's Ferry, Idaho, to Nelson, then were distributed from Goat River Landing, 20 miles east of Kootenay Landing. On the east side of the pass, supplies came from Lethbridge and were distributed from Fort Macleod.

P. Burns & Company established meat markets and distributing points at Fernie, Cranbrook, and Moyie. The C.Y. Ranch in the Territories had the contract to supply fresh beef to all camps from Lethbridge to Kuskanook. At first, beef was driven below the border and up into B.C., but when a proper road was established through the mountains, 60 beeves at a time were driven from the ranch to a supply base at Cowley. From there, five relays of three cowboys each drove right through the Crowsnest Pass, butchering at every camp along the way to ensure regular deliveries of fresh meat.

There was an art to driving the cattle so as to stop at the best grazing and holding grounds each day for food, water, and rest. When the cowboys arrived at a camp, they would ask the cook how many beeves he needed for two or three days, and would then kill, skin, and dress the meat right there on the ground. They hung the carcasses in improvised meat houses without fly-proofing or any sort of cold storage. Then they mounted up and drove the cattle on down the trail in a cloud of dust and flies.

Cutting ties for 330 miles of railroad was no small task. Most men made between 40 and 60 hand-hewn ties on a good day, but some of the old tie-hacks could make up to 70. Haney also commissioned a sawmill near Cranbrook. Logs would come from the CPR timberland acquired by Baker's charter. The CPR financed both the building of the mill and its equipment, including teams and supplies for logging.

Haney engaged the services of two bright young doctors to serve the medical needs of the construction camps. New to the Kootenay region, Dr. J.H. King and Dr. F.W. Green established a hospital at St. Eugene Mission near Cranbrook. Inexperienced as they were, neither suspected how far their commitment to their chosen profession would be tested.

As a rhythm of work was established, Haney's army began to run like the proverbial well-oiled machine. The track went south from Lethbridge, then west, following the Oldman River over prairie coulees that required extensive cuts and bridges. It passed Whoop-up and crossed the St. Mary River on a 2,933-foot-long trestle that swayed 65 feet above the ground. Reaching Fort Macleod, the steel swung west, continuing along the Oldman River toward Pincher Creek. Enthusiasm was high, despite long hours, plain food, an absence of washing facilities, and overcrowded sleeping cabins or tents. But the first payday was met with utter dismay when workers discovered they had been charged for blankets, and worse, their travel expenses were being deducted from their wages. Some owed more than they had earned, and received a bill instead of a payout.

The Welsh immigrant workers were most vocal in their anger. British farmers were not used to the rough conditions of railway construction, and the Welsh were not prepared to accept both low wages and poor camps. They demanded an explanation and were told that those employed by the CPR were only charged transportation from Fort Macleod to their place of work. The CPR charged each contractor one cent per mile, totalling approximately $22.50 for the trip from Ottawa, Montreal, or Winnipeg to Fort Macleod. The contractors had to deduct this charge from their workers' wages.

It was big money for workers earning only $1.50 a day. Some threatened

Below: *The CPR had 1,000 construction horses and 5,000 men working on the railroad through the Crowsnest Pass.*

to quit, and were reminded that they had signed a contract to work for the duration. If they quit, they would be arrested under the Master and Servant Law. The Welsh workers saw to it that the press got wind of their complaints.

When Van Horne and CPR vice-president Thomas Shaughnessy saw the newspaper coverage, they declared the situation an embarrassment to the company. Laurier was equally embarrassed. James Smart, the deputy minister of the interior, warned Laurier that if the situation was not corrected, "immigration to Canada could be very materially checked."[23]

Shaughnessy blamed Laurier's Alien Labour Law: "We can get plenty of navvies accustomed to railway construction, and it is only prejudicial to the cause of immigration to import men who come

here expecting to get high wages, a feather bed, and a bath tub. British labour is not suited either physically or psychologically to the conditions on the frontier."[24] Shaughnessy's view was no different from that of most Canadian businessmen of the 1800s, who preferred physically strong, non-unionized workers unable to use the English-Canadian press to focus public attention on their grievances. Van Horne told Smart that it would be "a huge mistake to send more immigrants from Britain for work on the Crowsnest line."[25] No more British immigrants were hired.

As the railway pressed on toward the Rocky Mountains, the Oldman River's course was altered three times to accommodate it. Continuing west, the track crossed the south fork of the river, requiring another long trestle measuring 840 feet. Undulating prairie rose and folded into foothills, and the track wound its way through them, a sinuous silver ribbon mounting steadily on its approach to the eastern gateway of the Crowsnest Pass.

Instead of improving, camp life grew steadily worse. Haney's attitude was that if the labourers were unhappy, they should work faster and harder, the sooner to be done. Twelve- and fourteen-hour shifts were already common, and on urgent jobs some men worked 48 hours straight, stopping only for meals. The construction workers were making incredible progress and showed great spirit toward the project, but there were many complaints about charges for mail fees, overcharges for supplies by some of the contractors, the plain, repetitive diet, and the lack of proper washing facilities. Mosquitoes tortured workers all summer. A plague of lice and other undesirables spread throughout the camps. Summer turned to autumn, and with autumn came killing frosts. The mosquitoes died and the days were more pleasant, but the nights grew unbearably cold and the joints of Haney's well-oiled machine stiffened with rheumatism.

Only one-tenth of the French Canadians could read English and understand the contract they had signed. They began refusing to work, so they were arrested and made to serve short jail terms before being returned to the line. Some escaped and fled back east, on foot with no money. One inspector pleaded their case to Sam Steele: "The agent in Ottawa hired these French Canadian axe men as choppers for bush work, but they were put to work instead with a pick and shovel. Very few have ever handled a pick, shovel and scraper. They naturally get into trouble and in a great many cases refuse to do work they did not engage to do and cannot do, and then we are called upon to compel them or send them to jail. They are forced to sleep in the open, often without blankets on the ground, or in cold and filthy houses, boxcars or hoarding cars. These men are completely discouraged and do not much care what happens to them."[26] He refused to arrest any more men who could not read the contract.

A fervent sense of brotherhood in a great work contributed to order in the camps, but as tension and despair mounted there were turbulent bouts of hard drinking, quarrels, fights, even murders. With a firm hand the NWMP patrolled the Alberta side of the Crowsnest Pass line from Fort Macleod and, in November 1897, the B.C. government extended their mandate to act as police authority along the B.C. section.

The NWMP kept law and order on the Crow's Nest Pass Railroad construction line in B.C. and Alberta.

To enhance their authority, members were sworn in as special B.C. police officers.

While the railroad construction workers suffered, the fruits of their labour brought good times to local merchants. Hotels were hard pressed to accommodate the large number of men arriving in the area. Prairie farmers didn't know whether to curse or celebrate as they struggled to keep up with feeding some 5,000 hungry construction men and providing tons of hay and grain to be consumed by 1,000 teams of horses. Ranchers prospered as meat markets handled from 300 to 400 cattle a month. The Crow's Nest Pass Railroad was hailed by the *Macleod Gazette* "as one of the most important public works in the history of the Dominion."[27]

Towns blossomed or withered according to which direction the nourishing stem of the railway bent. Who would be graced with the abundance it brought, and who would be left in the cold? Pincher Creek was one of the first to be slighted. The rail bypassed it by a couple of miles. Bellevue and Coleman would not be born for several years, not until the coal mines were developed.

Fernie was one of the first new towns to appear when William Fernie started his mine at Coal Creek, bringing in 20 hand-picked Cape Breton coal miners. Hillcrest, Frank, Blairmore, Crow's Nest, Michel, Hosmer, Corbin, Morrissey Mines, Elko, Jaffray, Kimberley, Swansea, Moyie, Moyelle, Yahk, Kitchener, Erickson, Sirdar—all sprang up on the map, contending for positions as potential cities. Cranbrook and Fort Steele eyed each other and waited.

A flurry of speculation accompanied the CPR's negotiations with landowners for a location to establish the B.C. Southern's divisional headquarters and main station in the region. As the new transportation hub, the chosen town's rise to prominence and prosperity was guaranteed. The natural choice—the expected choice—was Fort Steele on the Kootenay River, already central to the established traffic flow. Fort Steele was the first town in the southeast Kootenay region and the district's seat of government. The town was enjoying a boom: large hotels and businesses had been erected and hundreds of prospectors' tents were pitched on the outskirts of town. Livery stables were hopping, as freight was hauled with four-horse teams and people travelled by stage, in hacks, buckboards and buggies, or on horseback. Freight and passengers also arrived on the several boats running between Jennings, Montana, and Fort Steele.

Robert Galbraith projected confidence when he demanded a fair price from the CPR for Fort Steele land, but the shrewd Baker undercut Galbraith by offering free land on his Cranbrook estate. He donated every second lot, amounting to half the town, thus enticing the CPR at the 11th hour to build the B.C. Southern's main station and divisional headquarters at Cranbrook. So began the downfall of promising Fort Steele.

But its fate had actually been sealed years before, when Baker and Van Horne fell into step with their vision of a railroad through the pass. Baker's B.C. Southern had entered into early private negotiations with the CPR. And Robert Galbraith had secured Fort Steele's downfall back in 1888 when

Robert Galbraith's family founded Galbraith's Ferry on the Kootenay River. His land speculations led to the downfall of the town.

he invested in Baker's townsite company, which placed him in a position to benefit if the CPR chose Cranbrook over Fort Steele. Baker's company had enjoyed brisk sales of lots in Fort Steele to merchants and speculators when it was widely believed that it would be chosen. Then, with the CPR's announcement that it would build on the flat meadow of Joseph's Prairie, a mass exodus carried the land boom south to Cranbrook. The townsite company set up a real estate office near Baker's store. Galbraith had failed publicly, but in private he grew fat, alongside Baker, from land sales in both towns.

In September, the Crow's Nest Pass Agreement became law. The following month, three months after construction began, CPR officials and railways minister Andrew G. Blair signed the official government contract with the CPR for building the British Columbia Southern Railway. It stipulated that the line from Lethbridge to the south end of Kootenay Lake be completed by December 31, 1898.

Baker formed a new company with Cox and Jaffray, the Kootenay Coal Company, to negotiate coal measures with the CPR and Ottawa. Baker was elected president, Cox vice-president, and William Fernie, on-site director. The federal government entered into a tripartite agreement with the CPR, Kootenay Coal Company, and the B.C. Southern in which cash, company shares, and coal-bearing lands were traded all around. The Kootenay Coal Company agreed to develop the mines and supply coal to the CPR at a reasonable price.

As Baker signed, he may well have thought back to the day when he first envisioned a relationship of mutual benefit with the CPR. After 10 years of tireless lobbying, his vision had come to pass. The bush was being cleared, the roadbed was being graded, and the steel was being laid toward the coal.

❖   ❖   ❖

To some extent, the manual hardships on the line were overcome as soon as trains were able to run. In places where earth needed to be hauled a long way, a track was laid and small one-yard dump cars were filled by hand shovels, then pulled by a single horse along the track. A work train supply service started as soon as the grade was wide enough to hold the ties and rails. Temporary skeleton bridges enabled steam shovels to be brought in to widen and complete the roadbed, and pile drivers to install permanent bridges.

As the railway progressed, the tie hackers kept up an amazing output of ties, engaging in friendly competition to push themselves to the peak of endurance. They were proud of the fact that their broad axes did not open the grain of the wood as saws did. This meant that their ties would absorb less moisture and last longer than saw-cut ties; but the CPR could not have met the soaring demand for ties without the sawmill. Orders flooded in for lumber and ties, piling and poles. The sawmill was expanded and got more equipment. Haney supplied whatever the mill required without hesitation, but he refused to supply even blankets for the men in the camps.

Under Lumsden's direction, the location survey was completed to Kootenay Landing at the south end of Kootenay Lake by November 1897. That same month, the two ends of the tote road met at Moyie Lake, but until the railway reached any given camp, that camp got along with the least possible supplies. Haney's suppliers worked as hard as the construction labourers to keep food and other necessities flowing. Appetites increased, however, with the long, gruelling hours and the advance of colder weather, and the labourers struggled to replenish their spent energy before falling into cold beds for what little sleep they could muster before first light found them on the line once more. Even with beef arriving every two or three days, camp cooks often ran out of beef and were mad as hell about it.

But even fresh meat was not enough to keep frozen, dirty, and exhausted men going at superhuman speed. Doctors Green and King made the rounds of their large territory by wagon or saddle horse over miles of rough construction roads and trails. They found that men had to sleep in unheated tents during the winter, or even on the ground without bedding, and had no way to dry their clothes. As a result they often suffered from colds and rheumatism. The doctors rode day and night to treat patients, then would head back to their office, only to be called out again. They responded as best they could, but they could not meet the needs of 5,000 men when cough, mountain fever, and diphtheria were sweeping through the camps.

Sanitary conditions were appalling, but moving the sick out of the camps was a problem. The doctors established several makeshift hospitals along the line, with beds made of pole frames and cedar-bough mattresses; cedar was supposed to repel lice. There were no nurses to assist, only flunkies to fetch water.

As the construction workers toiled on, newspapers continued to escalate the labour situation on the Crowsnest line throughout November and December. A Winnipeg Liberal MP, R.W. Jamieson, wrote Laurier in December, denouncing the "White Slavery" tactics of the CPR.[28] The Laurier government left matters to the CPR, who left matters to Haney. But when superintendents Steele and Deane reported the inhuman conditions to NWMP Commissioner Herchmer, who then summarized the reports to Fred White, the NWMP comptroller in Ottawa, White communicated the information to Clifford Sifton, the minister of the interior, and to the prime minister. Laurier was forced to pay attention.

At the same time, a Fort Macleod lawyer named Harris had taken up the cases of some of the French-Canadian workers and had sent a telegram to Laurier outlining the situation. Laurier asked Shaughnessy what was going on out there in the Crowsnest Pass. The CPR vice-president dismissed most of the workers' complaints, telling Laurier that the mayor of Fort Macleod "seems to have no information about the complaints that are being made, but … a designing lawyer seems to have got hold of the men and is endeavouring to play upon the feelings of yourself and other members of the government. I think we may feel sure that Haney will not permit the men to be unjustly treated."[29] Meanwhile, men were dying like flies from mountain fever in the makeshift facilities that failed to meet even their most basic needs for warmth and sanitary conditions.

Just when the doctors thought it could not get worse, typhoid hit and the St. Eugene Mission Hospital overflowed with patients brought in from the line. The doctors were torn between visiting the camps and tending the sick at the hospital. The death toll mounted and men complained bitterly about the inadequate medical care, for which they were being charged 50 cents per month.

By December the line from Lethbridge had been completed to within 12 miles of the Crowsnest Pass. As the calendar flipped to 1898, the deadline for completing the railroad became more tangible. Men threw themselves into their work with renewed vigour, regaining some of the original spirit that had compelled them to join: a sense of being part of something momentous and historic. The line leapt forward, penetrating into the pass, and Haney was pleased. He urged the contractors to continue pushing hard.

The suppliers pushed hard too. While track was speeding past the headwaters of the east-flowing Oldman River, high up in the pass, and advancing with heavy rock work along the shore of Crowsnest Lake, suppliers were frantically trying to stockpile enough food and building materials to last over the spring thaw, when roads would be impassable with mud and the camps would be cut off. C.E.D. Wood, the editor of the *Macleod Gazette*, visited the construction sites and wrote glowing accounts of the line's progress. Here is one report, dated January 14, 1898: "There are only about two months in which to freight most of the summer's supplies, as when the spring break up occurs it will be almost impossible to do any freighting for weeks. There are now about 200 teams on the road and about as many more are required."[30] Wagoneers ploughed through drifts, sometimes having to lead their teams on foot when the wind hurled broken crusts of snow as big as dinner plates and the horses would not face it.

Scurrying over the wintery roads along with the suppliers, the CPR doctors continued their hopeless struggle to keep up with sick cases. They had reached the point of exhaustion, and still the sick kept coming. Serious cases on the east side of the pass were sent to a private practitioner at Pincher Creek, but getting patients there was difficult. In one case, it took more than two days to get two men with diphtheria to Pincher Creek, and the practitioner sent for arrived "only in time to see them die."[31] His report prompted an investigation. The executive committee of the Winnipeg Trades and Labour Council requested that Laurier appoint a commission of three independent men to look into the treatment of labourers on the Crow's Nest Pass Railway. On January 15, the government appointed a three-man royal commission.

❖ ❖ ❖

As the investigation got underway, work went on in the windy Crowsnest Pass. Five miles past Crowsnest Lake, the track crossed the Continental Divide and achieved the summit at 4,580 feet, where Summit Lake flows into Michel Creek and is carried down the western slopes of the mountains. The track bore south with the creek for two miles, then bent north in a switchback descent that allowed the track to drop 200 feet without making the grade too steep. This section was

A track-laying machine like this one was used to lay ties and steel rails.

called the McGillivray (or Michel) Loop. The men had to contend with heavy gumbo mud that derailed the track-laying machine every few hundred feet. Every day brought new challenges and an increased sense of urgency. Although men were dying of sickness and poor living conditions, there had been no bad accidents yet. Considering the difficult terrain and the number of men, some very inexperienced, this was remarkable.

Most realized they had to look out for themselves if they hoped to survive. The rock drillers would not work when the wind was gusty. The bridge crews also began refusing to work in high winds. Then one day in April, when most of the bridge crews deemed the winds too unsafe, one crew decided to keep working. Their trestle over the St. Mary River near Lethbridge collapsed, killing three workers and injuring several others. "A strong wind was blowing," reported Cranbrook's *Herald*,

"and while a number of men were working up the bridge a portion of the structure gave way, throwing several of them to the ground a distance of fifty or sixty feet. The injured were quickly conveyed to a car and brought to the Lethbridge hospital ... The trestle, over 200 feet long, collapsed like a pack of cards and without warning."[32] When the accident occurred, a big fellow from the stricken bridge, his hair long and wild from six months of roughing it, went on a panic run to the next camp. "I'm killed, I'm killed!" he yelled, his mind broken by the terrible thing he had seen.[33]

The next bad accident occurred during the building of one of the highest trestles on any CPR line. Two men stood on scaffolding to saw off the tops of pilings about 100 feet high. A cable holding the scaffolding broke. Both men plummeted to their deaths.

In April, the survey of the west shore of Kootenay Lake was completed. The railway continued its descent along Michel Creek toward the Elk River. Break-up came, and with it high water. Torrents of snowmelt rushed down the mountains, swelling creeks and rivers. Work became even more dangerous and difficult, but miraculously there were no cases of drowning. High water significantly damaged a new sawmill the CPR had just completed along the Elk River, a little west of Fernie. Some newly built bridges were washed out and had to be rebuilt.

The royal commissioners reported on April 30. They found camp conditions to be lamentable. Living quarters were overcrowded

This giant trestle bridge over the St. Mary River near Lethbridge collapsed like a house of cards in a gust of wind, killing three construction workers.

and unsanitary, with 50 to 60 men occupying bunkhouses measuring only 24 by 40 feet each, with less than 7-foot ceilings and no ventilation. The commissioners also substantiated the "well-founded universal complaint concerning medical attendance. The men complained bitterly of the length of time that elapsed between the different visits of the doctors in the camps, and when in some instances attendance was needed in the case of broken limbs, fever, and attacks of diphtheria, the medical assistance could not be obtained within a considerable time."[34]

Many men had not been able to save anything even after many months of working, because the fare from eastern Canada to Fort Macleod and then from Fort Macleod to the work site was deducted from their pay. In addition, the CPR charged the regular fare of $64.40 to workers returning home to eastern Canada. Many did not have enough money to pay this large sum. Moreover, if a worker left his job before his contract expired, he was "liable to arrest for desertion of his employment. Under such conditions," the commissioners stated, "he felt like a prisoner in a strange land."[35]

The commission applauded the CPR for raising the daily wage to $1.75 in February—although board had been raised to $5 a week—but it strongly urged that the wages be raised even more, to between $2 and $2.50, so that the men could build up some savings. They also recommended that men who had worked for three months should be reimbursed for their fare to the Crowsnest, while those working six months should receive either free return fare or a fare reduction.

Shaughnessy was extremely upset. "They are a commission of labour agitators! They have aroused bitter animosity against the company in almost every section of the country. The report is about as one-sided and unfair as it could be because no attempt seems to have been made by the commissioners to explain the conditions which must necessarily attach to frontier railway work, and they make no reference to the difficulties resulting from the unwillingness to work on the part of a good many of those who were carried west a distance of two thousand miles."[36] Shaughnessy was reluctant to counter the charge publicly, however, stating that it would only prolong the newspaper coverage. He blamed the matter entirely on Laurier's insistence that they forego experienced, hardened navvies for soft and inexperienced immigrants, and he sincerely wished that the CPR had built the railway without government aid.

Top: *Living quarters for the railroad labourers were overcrowded and filthy, with 50 to 60 men occupying bunkhouses measuring only 24 by 40 feet each, with less-than-seven-foot ceilings and no ventilation.*

Bottom: *Those living in portable camps had to sleep in unheated tents during the winter, or even on the ground without bedding, and had no way to dry their clothes. Many took sick and died.*

The CPR did not implement the report's major recommendations, other than to carry out its own investigation to determine "as accurately as possible" if there were any wages owed to workers. [37] The Crow's Nest Pass Agreement had created a cordial relationship between the CPR and the Laurier government, but the company's treatment of the workers building the railway severely strained this relationship.

Warmer, drier weather came, bringing forest fires. Some bridges were burned out and had to be replaced, but the men were more comfortable and the terrible sickness abated. In the absence of adequate medical care, camp cooks took it upon themselves to keep their camps healthy. They felt a sense of personal accomplishment if no one in their camp died from sickness.

Operations began on the first completed section from Lethbridge to Fort Macleod on June 15. Grading had reached Kootenay Landing, while track had been laid 118 miles west of Lethbridge and 12 miles beyond the western portal of the Crowsnest Pass to Sparwood, B.C. The steel pushed on, spanning the Elk River canyon by the end of June and shooting rapidly towards Fernie.

On July 12, the steel arrived at Fernie. That coal town really boomed for some time after the coming of the railway. Descending again in elevation after leaving Fernie, construction continued southwest along the Elk River to Elko, where many cuts and fills were required. From Elko the tracklayers swung northwest.

Steel hit the Kootenay River and followed it for 13 miles before crossing to Wardner in August, when the Kootenay water was lowering. Even then, the bridge crew worked in water up to their waists to get the track across as soon as possible. It was a massive undertaking, as the bridge required four spans and a 180-foot steel-arch swing span. There was a great rush because some of the contractors were finished their contracts and had to ship their equipment west to another rush job.

Wardner was lively with the steamboat service from Jennings, Montana, bringing new people in every day, and contractors, teamsters, and labourers hustled to and fro in a burst of activity as the end of the project drew near. The CPR began to offer some of the men positions as brakemen on the trains after track-laying was done.

On Tuesday, August 23, the railroad arrived at Cranbrook, with great ceremony. That same day, at three o'clock, the first train of cars passed over the Kootenay River bridge at Wardner. Conductor Lockhart had charge of the train, Hugh Brock was at the throttle, fireman Campbell stoked the furnace. Cranbrook hotels, stores, banks—all were open for business. Three days later, regular train service commenced. Construction crews worked around the clock raising the railway's sturdy and attractive plant on old Joseph's Prairie.

Construction of railway workshops began at Fort Steele in the autumn of 1898 in preparation for the promised spur line, but Fort Steele would never recover from losing the main line. It would later become a living museum of what was once a vibrant Wild Horse gold town of 1860s Kootenay, when Galbraith's Ferry was built to carry the miners across to the diggings and much wealth was taken from the creek in placer gold.

The route continued southwest from Cranbrook, sloping down toward one of the most beautiful and difficult sections of the railway. Moyie Lake, called the "Lucerne of the West" for its spectacular

The "Lucerne of the West," Moyie Lake was a beautiful but costly section of the railway. In some places the track perched a mere six feet from the water.

At the south end of Moyie Lake, workers had to blast a 650-foot tunnel through the rock. When they saw light at the end of it, they broke out a barrel of beer.

scenery, has steep banks that made laying rail extremely difficult and costly. Heavy rock work was needed to maintain the grade along the banks, where in some sections the track perched a mere six feet from the water. At the south end of the lake, the workers had to blast a 650-foot tunnel through the rock. When they saw the first daylight through the passageway, they broke out a barrel of beer. Travelling through the tunnel and southwest along Moyie River, the tracklayers then met extensive swamp lands, which came as no surprise—the name Moyie was derived from the French word mouillé, meaning wetlands. Progress slowed until they got back on solid ground. With the end looming steadily nearer, they bent their backs to the work, and pushed on toward Yahk.

At Yahk, only a few miles from the American border, the track straightened out due west through very rough country, reaching the treacherous Goat River canyon near present-day Creston. A covered timber bridge, 200 feet long, was laid across as the Goat River plunged

A heavy rock cut on the rail route through the Crowsnest Pass.

wildly through the deep gorge below. Heavy rock cutting on both sides maintained the gradient.

The steel veered north from there, following the eastern shoulder of the Kootenay River Valley to Kitchener, where prospecting was in full swing on the iron deposits. With the end in sight, track-laying pushed ahead with amazing speed and was completed to Kootenay Landing at the south end of Kootenay Lake that same day. Here, 4¼ miles of trestles, as well as a steel bridge, were required to cross the broad, marshy delta of the Kootenay River where it merges with the lake. Before tackling the work, the railway labourers waded into the cold waters and immersed themselves for the most long-awaited and refreshing bath of their lives. Then they completed the work, and the last spike was driven. It was October 5, 1898. The ballasters came behind, levelling and setting the track.

Thus, the Crow's Nest Pass Railway was complete, ahead of schedule. The CPR leased the B.C. Southern in perpetuity. Colonel Baker, after his 10-year struggle to see a railway through the pass, left it to others to develop the rich coalfields. He sold his holdings and retired to England in 1900. He died of heart failure on July 31, 1906, in Dorset, at age 76. His son Hyde continued to run the store in Cranbrook, and he became one of that town's most prominent citizens.

In the latter part of October, Van Horne took a party of friends and business associates on an inspection tour of the entire line. He reported to Baker later: "I was much impressed with what I saw between Kootenay Lake and the pass. All that you have told me about that district seems quite within the mark. It contains vastly more potential wealth than I imagined."[38]

On December 7, to celebrate the completion of its B.C. Southern through to Kootenay Lake, the CPR held an extraordinary party for 105 entrepreneurs and politicians. The VIPs were ushered aboard the sternwheeler S.S. *Moyie* for a gala excursion to Kootenay Landing, where they boarded a special train to Cranbrook. There they were lavishly banqueted, and when they could eat and drink no more, they spent the night in well-appointed sleeping cars. In the morning, they were whisked in style to Fernie over the shining new railway.

Construction of the railroad through the Crowsnest Pass from Lethbridge to Kootenay Landing had taken 18 months and averaged an incredible three miles every five days, including tunnels and bridges. The price tag was an estimated $9,898,392. Some men had paid with their lives. The persistence and dedication of men like Baker, Van Horne, and Haney are well documented, and their names will not be forgotten. But the Crow's Nest Pass Railroad was built with back-breaking labour against great obstacles, using the plainest tools, and that triumph belongs to the unsung thousands of construction workers, many of whom stayed on in the Crowsnest Pass region to live out their ordinary lives, raising families and settling the land. They are the real heroes of the railroad.

THE FRANK SLIDE

Frank Anderson

I t was late afternoon, April 28, 1903. Raoul Green took his eyes from the transit sight and squinted at the sun sinking into the V between Turtle and Goat mountains at the west end of the Crowsnest Pass. Five-thirty, he estimated, then checked his pocket watch as a matter of formality.

"It's five-thirty. Time to wrap it up," he called to his assistant, who was already moving the level to a new location. The boy telescoped the level and joined him.

"Where do you want to hide the equipment tonight, Mr. Green?" The surveyor glanced around at the bush and rocks, trying to decide upon a hiding place for their expensive instruments. Rather than pack the heavy equipment two miles back to Blairmore every night, they had been in the habit of concealing it in the underbrush, ready for service the next morning. He had almost chosen a suitable place when he stopped suddenly—he had a strange feeling.

Raoul Green's gaze moved from the valley to the mist-hidden crest of Turtle Mountain, towering 3,000 feet above them. A swirling grey mass of cloud was strung along the mountaintop like an untidy table-cloth.

"We'll take it back to the hotel tonight," he decided abruptly.

"But, Mr. Green, we always leave it …" The lad groaned at the thought of the two-mile hike along the railroad tracks to Blairmore.

"I know," Green answered, picking up the delicate transit. "But I've got a funny feeling. Tonight we're taking it back."

As they scrambled down the embankment onto the roadbed of the Canadian Pacific Railway, Green could not help glancing apprehensively at the mist that hid a series of massive rolls of limestone jutting outward above the valley. There was no real reason for his concern. True, an old Indian legend that the mountain moved was talked about by the ranchers and trappers, and it discouraged the Indians from camping at its base, but there had never been any indication that it was unsafe.

As the two men trudged westward along the tracks, they passed McVeigh and Poupore's construction camp—a dozen tents pitched on the right-of-way between the railway and Turtle Mountain. On their right, the valley rose sharply north toward the mining town of Lille, six miles away. The West Canadian Collieries had opened coal properties at Lille the previous year and constructed the Frank and Grassy Mountain Railway on a gradual but rather steep grade down from Lille to just north of Frank. The manager, J.J. Fleutot, had decided to extend this spur along the valley and join the CPR about a mile east of Frank, where six coke ovens had been built. McVeigh and Poupore had completed the main section of the line the previous October and were now waiting to begin work on the connecting link.

Directly behind the construction camp, the ground sloped gently toward the Oldman River, which flowed eastward through the Crowsnest Pass and along the base of Turtle Mountain. Ahead and slightly to the left of the CPR tracks sprawled Frank itself, separated from the rest of the valley by Gold Creek, which joined the Oldman under the shadow of the mountain.

Frank, North-West Territories—the region did not become part of the new province of Alberta until 1905—owed its existence to coal, which Henry S. Pelletier had discovered outcropping on Turtle Mountain in 1900. He sold his claim to Samuel W. Gebo, a promoter who had already established mining operations near Burmis, a small community to the east. Gebo,

Frank, nestled under the shadow of the mountain, shortly before the famous slide that would bury half the town.

backed by H.L. Frank of Butte, Montana, developed the find in the spring of 1901. The mine entrance was opened 45 feet above the river level and a spur line built from the CPR tracks. On the flats west of Gold Creek the company constructed 25 cottages, a large boarding house for single miners, and office buildings for their operation.

The nearest town with hotel accommodation was Blairmore, two miles to the west, which expected to enjoy a boom with the opening of the Frank mines. Owing to a land dispute among some of the original settlers at Blairmore, however, businessmen were reluctant to establish there. They looked to the Canadian American Coal Company for leadership, and Frank and Gebo acted promptly to attract business to their embryonic village. With a flair for showmanship, the two entrepreneurs decided that their venture should begin with a gala opening of the townsite on September 10, 1901.

On the day of the reception, the CPR ran two special trains—one from Lethbridge, the other from Cranbrook—to the west in British Columbia. The local newspapers in the area carried feature stories on the event, headlining the fact that the only expense would be rail fare, the rest was free. H.L. Frank missed his own train connection, but in true flamboyant style, hired an engine and caboose and overtook the eastbound special at Moyie, B.C. When he arrived at Frank, nearly 1,400 spectators were swarming over the flats.

In a lavish ceremony that saw Sir Fred Haultain, Premier of the North-West Territories and A.E. (Arthur) Sifton, Territorial Treasurer, making proud speeches that everyone promptly forgot, the little mining community was launched. Following the formal opening, there was a lacrosse game between Lethbridge and Fernie and a football game between Blairmore and Pincher Creek. There were foot races and sporting events with gold medals for the winners. Then the guests sat down to a lavish dinner in the open, for which a ton of fresh fruit and ice cream had been brought from Spokane. There were tours of the company cottages, designed to attract the more stable, married coal miner. There were even tours of the mine itself, which had already penetrated into Turtle Mountain for 1,250 feet.

When the day was over and the trains had gone, there was more than one miner and more than one businessman who had been impressed with the possibilities of the new community. Among them was a young Scot, Alexander Leitch, who had left his family at Oak Lake, Manitoba, to explore the business prospects of the Crowsnest Pass.

With an objective of 1,000 tons of coal a day, the mine began to forge ahead, sometimes recklessly ignoring safety rules and sound mining practice. By the spring of 1903 the miners had penetrated over 5,000 feet, ripping out seams of coal that varied from 13 to 15 feet wide. Frank now had a population nearing 600 who were served by an electric light plant, a waterworks system, and a two-storey school. In addition there were 4 hotels and some 16 other business establishments along a booming main thoroughfare called Dominion Avenue. Business lots sold from $400 to $600 apiece, while residential lots brought $250.

On that April 28 evening that Raoul Green and his assistant trudged along the railway tracks, the community was well on its way to prosperity and stability. Emphasizing the latter points was the laughter that Green and his assistant heard as spectators encouraged the local ball team at practice for its first game of the season. Green left the equipment in his room at the Alberta Hotel in Blairmore and went to the dining room for supper. It was 6 p.m. Much of Frank and upwards of 80 residents had only a few hours left to live.

In Frank, Ellen Thornley washed the last supper dish and set it on the shelf above the kitchen sink. In the front room of the house, which also served as a shoe shop, she could hear her brother, John, bidding goodnight to the last customer. She went outside to empty the dishwater and when she returned, her brother was waiting. "Ellen, what say we stay at the hotel tonight. Your train comes in early tomorrow."

"But it's still the same distance to walk," protested Ellen with a laugh.

"Oh, I was just thinking that it would be fun to spend your last night in Frank at a wicked hotel," he joked. "In any case, you wouldn't have to rush like mad in the morning."

Ellen agreed. She had just completed treatment for rheumatism at the Sulphur Springs Sanatorium at Frank and had planned to spend her last night quietly with her brother. But on John's whim she went cheerfully into the bedroom to pack.

As they left the shoe shop and walked toward town, they could hear the cheers from the ball game. They stopped to talk with friends and acquaintances enjoying the last of the lovely spring day. They crossed a wooden bridge over Gold Creek, then a rough footpath brought them to the livery stable, which housed some 50 horses used in dray work and in the mine. Robert Watt, the stable boss, and his assistant, Francis Rochette, were just completing their chores before going uptown. Next door was a small log cabin occupied by Alfred "Jack" Dawe and two friends from Wales. They passed the temporary clapboard house of William Warrington, a miner from Macdonald's Corners in Ontario. The Warringtons had four teenage children, and staying with them was Alex Dixon, a friend from their hometown. Near the Warringtons was another clapboard house, where six miners from Lancashire, England, lived. No one knew much about them except that they were bachelors.

Once past the houses, the path skirted a row of miners' cottages, then zigzagged through a clearing dotted with rocks and lodgepole pine stumps. At the edge of the clearing the path joined Dominion Avenue, the main business thoroughfare.

With its wooden sidewalks, dirt road, hitching racks, and false-front buildings, Dominion Avenue resembled a scene from the "Old West." D.J. McIntyre's hall boasted a good stage and piano and opened for concerts, theatricals, lodge meetings, dances, and church services. Farther along the street, Marks and Buchanan operated Crown Studios, a sign in the window boasting, "Our photographs will always whisper, Come Again." There were two restaurants: the Palm, which advertised "Meals at all Hours," and the Frank Café. Genial Harry Matheson, a groom of only four months, published the *Frank Sentinel* from his tiny newspaper office on Dominion Avenue. While the first issue had greeted the community on October 12, 1901, neither time nor practice had improved the editor's spelling or his stock of type.

At the top of the street, near the site of the new CPR station still under construction, was the Union Bank of Canada. On mine paydays the bank reportedly paid out upwards of $125,000 in American silver dollars. The bank manager, J.H. Farmer, obviously a man of caution, was reputed to have kept four loaded revolvers in his apartment above the bank. Beyond, Alex Leitch's Grocery and Furniture Store ran stiff competition to the Albert Mercantile Company Store. The Post Office was at the end of the street.

Despite its frontier appearance, Frank offered most of the luxuries of the day. A.V. Lang operated a ladies' ready-to-wear clothing store, while F. Thompson and J.J. Murphy catered to the men. Suits at

Murphy's ranged from $11 to $20, with the proprietor advising that it was "No trouble to show goods." H. Gibead with his Wines, Brandies and Whiskeys Store catered to the liquid needs of Frank, while on the next street Minister D.G. McPhail of Knox Presbyterian Church strove to combat the evils of Demon Rum. Those getting married could get a licence from watchmaker Alex Cameron, bring their children into the world with the services of doctors G.H. Malcolmson or Tom O'Hagan, and purchase milk "furnished from one cow" from J.S. Carter's Frank Dairy. Dr. W. Barratt Clayton fixed teeth, S.J. Beebe's Union Laundry supplied diapers, and K.M. Langdon insured the lives of Frank's townspeople. For disagreements there was even a barrister, T.B. Martin.

Travellers could stay at the Imperial Hotel, which boasted "the best $2.00 a day house in Alberta" with steam heat, electric light, and plaster throughout. To get plastered inside, one had only to visit the bar. There were three other hotels—the Frank, the Union, and the Miners.

It was the Frank Hotel that Ellen and John Thornley checked into at 6:30 p.m. Like its competitors, the hotel was already preparing for the nightly sessions of drinking, blackjack, and poker.

Despite its wooden sidewalks, dirt road, hitching racks, and false-front buildings, "Old West" Frank offered most of the luxuries of the day.

Meanwhile, John McVeigh, general manager of the McVeigh and Poupore construction camp, left the office tent and walked slowly toward the horse corral at the east end of the camp. He found Jack Leonard, stable boss for the outfit, at the corral. "Quite a mist over the Turtle tonight," McVeigh observed, nodding to the towering cliffs above.

"Yeah, can't see much of Gebo's lonely mountain," Leonard quipped. "Are the extra men and horses coming in Friday?"

"Yes. I think you should head over to Pincher Creek and buy more hay. The survey is just about completed and the Breckenridge and Lund crew will be joining us. We'll need plenty of hay for their teams."

Jack Leonard reached for his saddle and bridle. "In that case, I'd better get going before it's too dark to see the trail."

John McVeigh waited for his assistant to saddle up, then saw him off on the 30-mile ride before retracing his steps. On the way he checked with Joe Britton, a two-fisted brawler who was labour foreman. There were only a dozen labourers in camp that night, a skeleton crew of taciturn men who could not write their names—or preferred not to. Bookkeeper J.J. Scott listed them on the records as The Banton Kid, Olaf the Swede, or some similarly concealing name. As McVeigh talked with Britton, the men were coming from their tents and walking down the tracks toward Frank to sample the wares of the Imperial, Union, or Frank hotels. Sometime after midnight they would swagger back along the ties, in varying degrees of sobriety, richer or poorer from playing the cards, but all ready for a night's rest before another day of toil. Next day they would be joined by about 130 men from the Breckenridge and Lund Construction Company, who would move in to improve the grade of the CPR rail line.

McVeigh walked back to the office tent, noting that the night chill was already setting in, crisping the ground, which had thawed with the exceptionally warm weather of the past few days. Normally, he would have returned to the Alberta Hotel in Blairmore, where he lived with his wife and child, but they had gone to visit her parents near Calgary. His brother, P. McVeigh, and partner, J. Poupore, would normally have been with him, but they were away on business in Fort Macleod. With a last look at the almost deserted camp, McVeigh went inside and drew the flaps.

Fate is the hunter

NWMP Constable Robert Bruce Leard checked his uniform and equipment before stepping out into the crisp night air for his evening tour of duty. In his early 20s, Leard had been transferred to Frank in the fall of 1902. Together with his superior, Corporal Jack Allan, who was at Fort Macleod on a case, Leard was responsible for keeping order in the community. His self-inspection completed, Leard briskly walked the half-mile to Frank, conscious that the night was getting colder.

He slowed to a stroll as he reached his beat along Dominion Avenue, his leather heels clacking sharply. Though noise from the hotel bars would have convinced a stranger that mayhem was being committed every minute, Leard ignored it. It was still early in the evening. At the end of Dominion he found the footpath to the eastern flats and followed it to the row of miners' cottages—all brightly lit except the vacant one at the end of the row.

The Bansemers lived in the first house, closest to town. Carl, a native of Germany, had first settled in Nova Scotia, but the prospect of work in the west had brought him and his family to the Crowsnest Pass. While the black coal of the mine gave a living to the Bansemers, their real ambition was for a homestead. Shortly after arriving at Frank they had located one near Lundbreck, a hamlet to the east. Earlier that day, Carl and his two eldest sons, Rufus and Henry, had left for the homestead with a load of furniture. His wife, Annie, with their remaining seven children, remained at home.

As Leard passed the second house, he could hear Rosemary Leitch playing the piano. Originally from the Ottawa Valley, she and her husband, Alexander, had been lured by the glamour of the West. They had made their first stop at Oak Lake, Manitoba, in the 1880s. In partnership with his three brothers, Alexander had tried the flour-milling business, but in 1901 came west and decided to settle at Blairmore. The land dispute at Blairmore, however, and the opening of Frank with its promise of prosperity, brought him to the mining town. Not content with the cramped company cottage for his wife and seven children, Leitch had enlarged the kitchen and added a second bedroom for the boys. The family was one of the most respected in the community, active in church work and popular as guests.

The next house was occupied by Charles Ackroyd, a miner from

Montana, with his wife and 13-year-old stepson, Lester Johnson. Like many other families in Frank, the Ackroyds had known tragedy. His wife had been born in Wisconsin and married a hometown lad. Of their family of 13, 10 died in a smallpox epidemic, and in 1891 her husband was killed in a mine accident. She raised the three remaining children—Ida, Charles, and Lester—working to support them until her marriage to Ackroyd. With the discovery of coal and the opening of the Frank mines, Ackroyd had joined the northward stream of miners into Crowsnest Pass, bringing Lester with him.

Their neighbours in the fourth house, painted a cheerful red and white, were the Sam Ennis family. As well as working in the mine, Sam drove the coal dray delivering coal to the villagers. Besides himself and his wife, there were two boys and two girls, all under 10. Living with them was James Warrington, a brother of Mrs. Ennis who also worked in the mine. James was notable because of a black moustache of truly magnificent proportions that was the pride of the family and the envy of local young bloods.

John Watkins lived with his wife and three children in the fifth cottage. Like the majority of Frank's residents, Watkins had gravitated to Frank with the bad times. Of the children, Thomas could look forward to a life of coal mining, while the two girls, Fernie and Ruby, would probably marry miners and worry about cave-ins and explosions.

The sixth cottage was vacant, and in the seventh and last, the lights were already going out. Alfred Clark, a miner on the night shift, was in the habit of catching a nap before he left for the mine. His eldest daughter, Lillian, would soon be returning from work in the mine boarding house, whose lights could be seen to the west. The rest of his children—Charles, Albert, Alfred, Ellen, and Gertrude, whose ages ranged from 5 to 15—were already in bed.

Constable Leard paused when he arrived at this last cottage in the row. To his left, night was already reaching down to cover Tallon Peak and Goat Mountain. In the far distance beyond the railway track he could make out the lights of Alexander Graham's ranch house. The valley to the north was quiet. From the right, the river rushed musically through its rocky banks and the occasional sound of clanking mine machinery at the tipple across the stream reached Leard's ears. Between him and the base of the mountain were about 10 temporary dwellings. Although the coal company discouraged shack building, the rapid expansion of the village demanded emergency accommodation.

Among these temporary dwellings were William Warrington's home and its neighbouring cottage, where the six Lancashire miners lived. Beyond them in the darkness were the residences of Ben Cunes, George Williams, Dan Mitchell, and James Vandusen, who had arrived at Frank only a fortnight before. Originally intending to ranch on the prairie, Vandusen had heard of the building boom in Frank and decided to continue his trade as a carpenter before embarking on his plans to start a dairy farm.

In all, some 100 people lived in the valley on the southeast side of Frank between the railway and the river. Destiny, finances and wanderlust had led them across the world, pausing here, moving there. Regardless, fate had decreed that each would rendezvous with death at the base of Turtle Mountain.

Constable Leard continued his beat, passing between the livery stable and the log cabin occupied by Dawe and his Welsh miners. Leard had no inkling of the danger lurking above. Although the Indians talked about the "mountain that walked," there had never been any indication that it was unstable. A favourite pastime of the miners had been climbing Turtle Mountain for its panoramic view of the countryside. This night there was no wind through the pass, and the sky was hidden in darkness. The constable heard only the sound of rushing water, the metallic clinking from the mine entrance, and the distant murmur from Dominion Avenue.

At the railway tracks, Leard turned back toward town. The camp watchman was not in sight, but the boxcar of dynamite that was to be used for blasting the last link of the Frank and Grassy Mountain line stood apart on its siding, a safe distance from the town and camp.

Back in town, Leard patrolled the main street until the bulk of the miners, merchants, and girls had departed from the hotel bars. By midnight, the last of the construction workers had returned to camp and the village was quiet, except for the remaining few alcoholics and patient barkeeps. Leard walked back to the log cabin that served as office, jail, and barracks and went to bed.

Lillian Clark also went to bed, but not at home. Although she had never spent a night away from home in her life, her mother, for the first time, had told her that if she was working late she should not return to her family. Instead, she should stay overnight at the boarding house.

By such a quirk of fate, her life was to be spared.

Thomas Delap heard a dog howling as he worked in the electric light plant beside the river. He had only a month or so earlier brought his bride to Frank and would have preferred to have been at the hotel with her. But lips, however red, have to be fed, and his job entailed night work.

In the cabin beside the coal company livery stable, Alfred "Jack" Dawe stirred in his sleep, cursing his terrier for disturbing the night. Across the room, he heard the measured breathing of his two friends. They should all have been travelling eastward over the CPR tracks to catch a boat for Wales, but a snarl-up in ticket reservations had forced them to cancel their trip for one week more. Reservations or not, however, they intended to leave Frank by the end of the week.

In the Union Hotel, Charles and Robert Chestnut slept soundly. Had fate—and sailing reservations—decreed otherwise, they would have been sleeping in the log cabin by the stable. Instead they had been forced to remain in the hotel until the three Welshmen vacated it.

The night of April 28 became the morning of the 29th as the clock in the Graham family kitchen ticked a measured second. Ned Morgan watched the minute hand creep beyond the midnight mark and rose to leave. It had been a profitable day, selling a cow and a calf to his rancher neighbour.

"Won't you stay the night, Ned?" Mrs. Graham suggested. "We've plenty of room in the house."

"Thank you kindly, Mrs. Graham, but I've left my team down near the village," Morgan replied. "I'd better be getting back to them."

James Graham accompanied Morgan to the yard and took a last look round as his visitor departed. Here, nestled against the foot of Turtle Mountain, bordered by the Oldman River on the left, the CPR on the right, and the indistinct boundary of the village to the west, laid his dream—a dairy farm. With Frank growing steadily and with only one other serious competitor, it had seemed wise to locate in the valley. He could have picked any of a dozen choice sites, including one selected by farmer Alex Graham (no relation) near the cemetery. But he had preferred to settle by the river, where he was content—especially since his two sons, John and Joseph, who had served in South Africa during the Boer War, had returned unharmed.

Graham's only near neighbour at his riverfront location was

Andy Grissack, a gnarled old trapper who camped in a tent beside the Oldman winter and summer. He was a great favourite with the children because of his stories—some said greatly exaggerated—of the Lost Lemon Mine and hidden mountain trails. As Ned Morgan's footsteps faded, Graham checked the bunkhouse where Graham's two hired boys, the Johnson brothers, slept. As his own sons worked in the mine, the Johnsons looked after his growing herd. Both were asleep.

Soon Graham was also asleep, the ranch house an indistinguishable shape against the inky blackness of Turtle Mountain. Neither the ranch house, its occupants, nor the old trapper were to see dawn break.

Ninety million tons of rock

At midnight a quiet cluster of men began to assemble on the main street of Frank and greeted each other with the monosyllabic grunts of men facing night work. Alex Tashigan, the weigh-scale man, huddled in his sheepskin. At least he wouldn't have to go deep into the belly of the Turtle, since his work kept him on the mine tipple all night. Joseph Chapman, a veteran miner and foreman of the night crew, waited impatiently for his gang to assemble. His diminutive assistant, Evan "Halfpint" Jones, leaned against the office building.

They were soon joined by John Watkins, William Warrington, and Alfred Clark. Then Shorty Dawson, Dan McKenzie, Alex McPhail, and Alex Grant came out of the shadows to huddle in the chill air and wait for the others. Talkative Charlie Farrell swung into sight, and finally, the 20th and last crew member shuffled out of the darkness.

Chapman checked them and led the way toward the mine tipple. Although he was ostensibly foreman of the night crew, in effect each man knew his job and needed no supervision. They crossed the mine bridge over the Oldman River and made their way up the gentle slope to the entrance.

About the same time, Robert Lloyd Watt and Les Ferguson came out of the Imperial Hotel and stretched their legs and backs after a session of blackjack. "I'll walk you back to the bridge, Bob," Ferguson said. "On second thought, why don't you stay with me at the hotel tonight?"

"Thanks, Les, but I think I'll turn in at the stable. See you tomorrow."

They parted on the sidewalk of Frank—Les Ferguson to return to his hotel room, Robert Watt to the eastern flats.

Perhaps as he walked, Robert Watt thought of his children in Lanark, Ontario. At 18, he had met and married Mary Ann Macdonald, a young widow with two children. With the smoke of the Riel Rebellion of 1885 still darkening the sky, the Watts had settled on a homestead in Manitoba to raise cows, grain, and children. Before her death in 1902, Mary had borne him seven children, six of whom survived her and were living in the East. Eleven years of trying to wrest a living from the poor soil on their homestead had become less attractive, and in 1896, the Watts returned to Lanark.

On Mary's death, Robert had been forced to seek work wherever it was to be found. When a job as mine carpenter and stable boss at Frank came to his attention, he snapped it up, leaving his children with relatives. If the job proved steady, he planned to send for his children. Watt checked the barn and looked in on his assistant, Francis Rochette, before climbing the stairs to his own sleeping quarters.

Meanwhile, an extra freight train from Fort Macleod was puffing slowly up the steep grade from Passburg to Frank, slowing from its customary speed of 25 mph to a labouring 10. At the throttle, veteran engineer Ben Murgatroyd scanned the darkness, alert to any danger. The Crowsnest Pass run was notorious for its broken rails, snow slides, and other pranks of nature which could quickly derail the clumsy Mogul engines. Fireman Bud Lahey stoked the ravenous boiler between checking the water gauge.

In the caboose, conductor Henri Pettit checked his train orders. They were far behind schedule because of a snowstorm just outside Fort Macleod and still had a lot of work to do, including picking up coal cars at Frank and a bridge piledriver. Above him in the gondola, caps tilted over sleepy eyes, brakemen Sid Choquette and Bill Lowes rode the jolting seats with the practised relaxation of long-time railway men.

When they reached the boxcar that served as a station at Frank, conductor Pettit checked with the local agent, T.B. Smith. The passenger train that shuttled between Dunmore Crossing, near Medicine Hat, and Kootenay Landing was running an hour and a half behind schedule, also delayed by the snowstorm. It was time-tabled to reach Frank about 4:30 that morning, and the freight would have to lie over on the siding until it passed.

After spotting the train on the siding, Pettit sent the engine and crew to the mine to pick up the coal cars. Then he parked his feet beside the pot-bellied stove in the station and listened to the intermittent clatter of the telegraph key.

At the mine tipple Sid Choquette and his companion hooked up the coal cars, then momentarily chatted with Tashigan, the weigh-scale man, and Fred Farrington and Alfred Clark, two miners who had come out of the mine entrance for their 4:00 a.m. lunches. Just below, in the darkness beside the river, they could see the lights of the boiler-house where engineer Thomas Delap tended the power plant. Beyond the river, the valley was in total darkness. To the left, they could see the lights of hotels in Frank, where clerks were already waking guests who would be travelling west on the passenger train from Dunmore Crossing.

After hooking the coal cars and the piledriver to their train, Ben Murgatroyd and his crew switched onto the mine spur again and backed up to the tipple to spot a solitary coal car. Tashigan and the two miners were still eating their lunches.

Thankful that their chore was nearly at an end, Choquette set the brakes of the coal car and pulled the connecting pin between the car and the engine. The Mogul began to roll slowly forward down the inclined track toward the mine bridge. Choquette and his fellow brakeman, Lowes, trotted alongside the slow-moving engine, flapping their arms against the intruding cold.

Far above, a huge rock shivered, fell forward, and bounded down the heavily wooded mountain. Then another toppled, impelled by some unseen force. Then another, and another.

Murgatroyd, a veteran of more than one close call on the treacherous mountain run, took no chances. Screaming a warning to the walking men, he rammed the throttle home and the Mogul churned forward on its metal wheels. Choquette and Lowes sprinted for the handrails and clung hard while the engine picked up speed on the grade.

Engineer Murgatroyd's quick action saved all their lives. There was a horrendous sound high above them, like a mighty clap of thunder. Ninety million tons of rock broke away from Turtle Mountain. As it plummeted down the precipitous slope, a blast of freezing air raced before it.

Like a screaming juggernaut, the rock careened down the mountainside. It swept over the mine entrance, erasing it entirely, then crashed against the mine tipple and hurled Clark, Farrington, and Tashigan into eternity. It caught the blacksmith shop and the solitary railway car and flung them two miles across the valley, twisting the mine-spur tracks like threads of silk. Seconds after the racing engine and its horrified crew cleared the bridge, the rocks hit one end of the wooden superstructure. Icy water sprayed high into the air as the bridge swung sideways, then subsided into the river. By then, however, the massive avalanche of rocks was already far across the eastern flats.

Ahead of the deadly rockfall, a solid wall of air toppled the flimsy houses, shacks, and tents and hurled men, women, and children hundreds of yards. Those asleep had no time to waken. Those awake never knew what was happening. Behind the wind came the churning, grinding mass of rocks that made the night cataclysmic with noise and streaks of fire as massive boulders leaped and clashed with each other.

The power plant was obliterated in an instant and the seething mass hurtled onto the valley floor, splaying like a fan. The main stream of rocks shot ahead, smashing the remains of the temporary dwellings,

The Townsite of Frank, Alberta, before the 1903 rock slide.

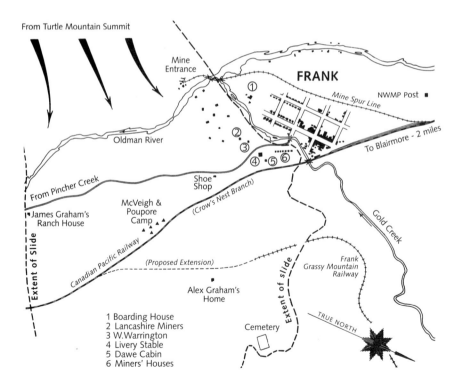

From Turtle Mountain Summit

Mine Entrance

FRANK

NWMP Post ■

① Mine Spur Line

Oldman River

To Blairmore - 2 miles

② ③

From Pincher Creek

④ ⑤ ⑥

Shoe Shop

(Crow's Nest Branch)

James Graham's Ranch House

McVeigh & Poupore Camp

Canadian Pacific Railway

(Proposed Extension)

Gold Creek

Frank Grassy Mountain Railway

Extent of Slide

Alex Graham's Home

Extent of slide

TRUE NORTH

1 Boarding House
2 Lancashire Miners
3 W.Warrington
4 Livery Stable
5 Dawe Cabin
6 Miners' Houses

Cemetery

cascading over the livery stable and Dawe's cabin, the construction camp, and the boxcar of dynamite before expending itself over the farm of Alex Graham and the cemetery. Another spur shot eastward, cascading over the James Graham dairy farm, the bunkhouse, and the two-storey farmhouse, burying the buildings and all occupants 50 feet deep. At the same time, the slide covered Gold Creek. It pushed an icy wall of grey mud ahead of it and sent it crashing against the row of miners' cottages on the outskirts of Frank. A 500-ton boulder jumped the creek and spun to rest within the village itself.

One hundred seconds after its plunge, the cataclysm of rocks had ploughed across the valley and 500 feet up the opposite slope beyond the tracks. Over the scene, a swirling mass of grey dust hung like a shroud.

It was 4:10 a.m., April 29, 1903.

Joseph Dobeck, who was oiling engines in the train shed 600 feet from the disaster, felt the earth shake and heard the monstrous noise. He stepped outside and peered eastward but could see nothing in the darkness. With a shrug, he returned to his job.

"Mormon Bill," a well-known local character, was standing on the street in front of the Miners' Hotel, cooling off after a strenuous night of poker. He was rocked on his feet by the blast of wind and heard the din. In less than two minutes all was still. Although all around him men and women were rushing into the streets in their night attire, Bill pulled himself together, attributed the sensations to too much liquor, and went home to his shack to sleep soundly.

John Anderson, a more sedate and methodical man who had gone to bed at a respectable hour, was awakened by a hurricane wind that shook his house from shingles to sub-cellar. Bounding to the window, he saw a few feet away what he thought was a cloud of smoke cascading past his house. Unaware that the smoke was actually a hurtling sea of limestone, Anderson waited until the din ceased. Then he returned to bed, little knowing that in the morning he would look through the same window in utter disbelief.

At the same time, Ellen Thornley was thrown from her bed at the Frank Hotel and unceremoniously dumped on the opposite side of the room as the building rocked from the gigantic force. When she regained her composure, she dressed hurriedly and ran downstairs to find the street in confusion. People were crying that the end of the world had come, others ran from the direction of the unearthly burst of noise. A woman carrying a small child, both in nightclothes, ran toward her. Ellen whipped off her heavy coat and wrapped it around them. With hurried thanks, the woman and child fled, away from Gold Creek and the eastern flats.

One hundred miles north, near Cochrane, two young men who had just taken their girlfriends home after a date reined in their team. Both had heard what they thought was the sharp report of a giant rifle being fired in the mountains to the south. They checked their watches. It was 4:10 a.m. "Somebody must be having a real party down there," one joked, as he stirred the horses into a trot.

When day broke over the Frank Slide, people cried that the end of the world had come. Survivors salvaged bodies from the rubble as the remains of the back row of miners' cottages burned.

Constable Leard, startled out of sleep by the reverberations, raced to the station. He questioned some of the people milling in the street but no one knew what had occurred. That there must have been an explosion of gigantic proportions at the mine was the most obvious answer. Leard's first thought, knowing the scanty resources of the village, was to call for help from outside.

He found the train crew stunned. Even then, though they had escaped by the length of a bridge, engineer Murgatroyd and his men had no idea of the magnitude of the catastrophe that had almost engulfed them. That something unusual had occurred could be determined by the rumbling rocks and trembling earth, but darkness shielded the extent of the disaster.

Even as Leard arrived at the station, the two brakemen, Choquette

and Lowes, were setting out across the rocks to flag down the passenger train, expected within 20 minutes. After learning that the east telegraph line had gone dead, Leard started the wires humming toward Cranbrook in British Columbia, the first major town west of Frank.

Unaware of the magnitude of the slide, Choquette and Lowes plunged into the massive mound of rocks, some still hot from their 3,000-foot skip down the mountain. Their trainman lanterns were little use against the darkness, now mixed with a cloud of grey dust. In astonishment they groped their way around rocks so huge they couldn't see the top. Lowes, short of breath, gave up, but Choquette scrambled on, growing more aware that this was no ordinary rock slide. When it seemed that the slide would never end, Choquette found himself on its eastern edge, right where the eastbound tracks emerged from the slide.

A few minutes later, clothes and shoes scarred, breath laboured, Choquette flagged down the passenger train as it rolled through the

Only the bravery of Sid Choquette prevented this passenger train from slamming into a solid wall of rubble. The passengers disembarked, little suspecting the devastation that lay ahead.

darkness. His action saved another possible disaster. If the train had slammed into the slide, more lives could have been lost. Both he and Lowes risked their lives, since neither knew if a second rockfall would follow the one that had almost been their memorial.

Death and destruction

George Bond, a traveller from Ottawa, was in bed at the Union Hotel when the hurricane wind hit the frame structure. The hotel was violently shaken and seemed to writhe on its foundation. When the movement subsided, Bond leapt into his clothing and ran downstairs. Already, lights were going on in homes and people were dazedly emerging onto the streets.

Once outside, Bond noticed that a fire had started about 600 feet to the east, across Gold Creek. In company with others, he raced toward it, conscious that somewhere ahead was the sound of rocks tumbling down a mountainside. Since the creek had been rerouted to the west by a wall of mud, he and his companions had to wade the stream. Through the dust-laden air they saw the ruins of several houses, two of which were burning.

A tongue of mud and rocks had broken away from the main body of the slide and played a deadly game of chance with the dwellings. At the extreme eastern end, the cottage of Alfred Clark had vanished completely, along with his wife and five children. The Watkins home was a broken hulk of shattered timbers and boards; the Ennis residence, once a proud red-and-white cottage, lay in ruins; the Ackroyd home was crushed and burning; the Leitch house, sliced in two at the eaves, was almost demolished, the top half having been carried by the rocks and mud to the bank of the creek. The only building reasonably intact was Carl Bansemer's, which had been pushed several feet off its foundation. Debris around the doors and windows blocked all exits.

Attracted to the Ennis home by cries for help, rescuers found that Sam Ennis had extricated himself and was trying to free his wife, Lucy, who was pinned by a beam. Lights were brought from the village and the rescuers dug into the cold mud and slime to release the imprisoned victims. Despite painful injuries, Lucy Ennis had already managed to save the life of her infant daughter, Gladys, who had been sleeping with them. The child had almost suffocated from having her

By 1903 the Alfred Clark family included five children. Only Lillian, right, survived because she was at work.

mouth blocked by a clod of earth, which Lucy was able to remove.

Shaken but intact, Ennis helped rescue his three other children before faint cries attracted them to the back room of the house where James Warrington had been sleeping. As they freed him, Warrington warned that he could feel something soft beneath him. Digging carefully, the men located Mrs. Watkins, who had been flung from her cottage next door. She was pulled from the rubble suffering from shock and countless rock splinters that made her skin look like a pincushion.

Mrs. Ennis had a broken collarbone, and Warrington a broken upper thigh. Apart from assorted cuts and bruises, the children had miraculously escaped major injury. In the darkness where the Watkins cottage had stood, the two teenage children, Ruby and Thomas, pulled themselves from the rubble and looked around. There was no sign of their sister, Fernie. Then somewhere in the darkness a man began to call. Stumbling through the cloud of dust, the youngsters fought through the jagged rocks to the voice, but they no longer heard the man calling. Already water had backed up from the Oldman River, which was partly dammed by the slide, and Gold Creek, which was blocked and had to find a new route, but they managed to wade the waist-deep chilly water and reach safety.

They did not know what had happened. Nor did they know where their mother or baby sister were, and little suspected that their father and the rest of the night crew were trapped deep inside the mine.

Lester Johnson had felt the wind lift their house a couple of feet off its foundation. Scarcely had it settled when there was a shuddering crash and the house toppled onto them. He heard his parents scream.

He remembered nothing more until he revived to find himself lying between two enormous boulders that had crashed together over him, pinning him but sheltering him from the onslaught of falling rock. Through the haze of dust, he could see that day was breaking and that fires were burning a short distance away. He tried to crawl toward the light, but a piece of lath that had been driven into his side caught on the rocks. He fainted.

When Lester regained consciousness, it was broad daylight and the dust had settled considerably. Through the opening between the rocks he could see Sam Ennis and others digging in the ruins of the Leitch home. He managed to break the lath and pull it from his side and crawl into the open. His nightclothes had been torn from his body and he emerged from his rock-womb like a newborn babe.

Nearly frozen, he managed to swim the creek and make his way to the Williams family, who were so excited that no one noticed his

The Oldman River and Gold Creek were affected by the Frank Slide. The Watkins children had to wade the waist-deep chilly water to reach safety.

nakedness or his wound. When Mrs. Williams examined him, she found feathers where the lath had driven through the mattress and penetrated his body. They bundled him into blankets and in an old iron wheelbarrow trundled him to Dr. Malcolmson's hospital. For the third time Lester passed out—this time from warmth and sleepiness.

Dr. Malcolmson's living room had been converted into a hospital ward because the regular ward beside the house was already full. He plucked feathers from Lester as he would have from a chicken. Shortly after, when Mrs. Watkins was brought in, the doctor switched from plucking feathers to prying out stone splinters.

In the ruins of the Leitch home, silence prevailed as George Bond and his fellow workers approached after freeing the Ennis family. By then day was breaking. Though the top had been sheared off the house and carried along with the crest of the slide, the remainder of the three-room house lay in a mess of collapsed walls. The rescue party found an opening in the rear and crawled into the back room. Here

Of more than 100 people in the path of the slide, only 23 survived. Here are 7 of them, the Sam Ennis family, in front of a tent donated after their home was destroyed. Standing with the crutch is Jim Warrington, who had been staying with them.

they found two girls, Jessie and Rosemary (May), pinned on the bed beneath a ceiling joist. They were unharmed and soon passed to safety. But the rescuers' relief at finding the girls alive soon turned to grief. In the next room beneath the mud and plaster they found the bodies of two of the four boys. In a third room, they unearthed the bodies of Alex Leitch and his wife. The remaining two boys, buried even deeper in the debris, were not found until the following day.

The Leitches' baby daughter had had an astounding escape. She had been flung from the demolished house and landed on some hay that had been whisked from the destroyed livery stable. Mrs. Bansemer, hearing the child's cry, directed searchers until the baby was found.

Fernie, the third of the Watkins children, also had a miraculous escape. She too had been tossed from her house and was lying cold and dirty behind some rocks when found by pit boss Edgar Ash.

As morning broke over the valley, the searchers began to appreciate for the first time the magnitude of the disaster. The evening before, the sun had set on a peaceful scene; it rose now to reveal a river of rocks a mile and a half wide and over a mile long, fanning out from the base of the mountain. Above, where there had been a steep, heavily wooded slope, there was only a jagged slash on the mountain. Below the break, rocks still tumbled downward in clouds of grey limestone dust. The river, which had coursed safely through its rocky banks, was flooding rapidly, creating a lake and backing into Gold Creek.

The searchers gazed with horror upon the sea of rock as they realized there was no hope for the 50 or more men, women, and children who had lived on the eastern flat beyond the row of cottages. Those not killed outright were now trapped and faced certain drowning.

At the eastern edge of the slide, James Graham's log house was buried beneath a hundred feet of rock. Somewhere under the massive mound he lay with the bodies of his wife, sons, and the two Johnson boys. They found the old trapper, Andy Grissack, wrapped in his tent with an iron frying pan clutched in his hand. When the searchers rolled him over, his scalp peeled like a layer of onion skin.

To the north of the farm of Alex Graham, dusty grey boulders, some still covered with the original shale and brush from the mountaintop, lay deathlike and still. Neither his body nor that of his wife was ever found.

Behind the farm, the cemetery lay almost completely buried. To the west of the cemetery, rails from a section of the Frank and Grassy Mountain rail line were twisted grotesquely and ties slivered into fragments of wood. Along the CPR tracks, rock piled three times the height of a train marked where John McVeigh, Joe Britton, J.J. Scott, and their 12 construction labourers lay buried.

Somewhere on the eastern flats under the mass of rocks, George Williams, his wife, and four children rested, as did his brother-in-law, Thomas Lock. The entire Vandusen family of four were gone, as were Mrs. William Warrington, her four children, and their visitor, Alex Dixon. The cottage beside theirs containing the six Lancashire miners had vanished. The Ben Cunes family of four, together with 10 or more unknown miners, lay covered by the death-dealing blanket of rocks.

A rumour persists that at least 50 men hoping to get work in the mine had arrived in Frank the evening before and pitched tents on the recreation field. While some old-timers insist that they were there and must have perished, others believe they had gone on to Blairmore. The truth lies beneath the rocks.

The body of Fred Farrington, who had been eating his dinner on the mine tipple, was found a quarter-mile away on the western edge of the slide. No trace of his dinner companions, Tashigan and Clark, was ever found. The body of Thomas Delap, the newlywed engineer at the electric light plant, was not found for days; it was then discovered only a short distance from the plant.

Where the livery stable had stood at the foot of the row of miners' cottages fate again had been inconsistent with bodies. Robert Watt, who had been sleeping in the loft, was never found. The body of his assistant, Rochette, was located lying in rocks, looking almost as if asleep. Throughout the whole area, the bodies and broken limbs of horses were scattered in profusion.

The log cabin beside the stable was gone and with it the two Welsh miners. The body of the third occupant, Alfred Dawe, was found near the railway station. Astonishingly, his faithful fox terrier was uninjured and was found wandering and whining near where the cabin had stood.

As dawn broke over the stricken town, a citizens' meeting was held and search parties organized. One group, which had been stumbling in the dangerous dark of the mountainside trying to locate the mine

This massive boulder was part of the slide debris.

entrance, gazed with disbelief upon the sheared-off surface. The slope above was a seething sea of stone, huge masses of rock still breaking away from the crumbling rim above. The mine bridge over which the locomotive had raced with inches to spare lay twisted and broken in the icy, rising waters.

While the mine engineer sought to pinpoint the entrance with his transit, men spread over the rocks, collecting timber for a raft to cross the river. A rope was strung from bank to bank and the makeshift raft began to shuttle men and equipment to the wounded slope. Amidst still-falling rocks, they began their assault to free the trapped miners.

Considering the damage to the mine entrance, however, it seemed impossible that any of the men inside would be alive. Nevertheless, the rescuers kept at their task, more from habit than hope. While some watched the slope above to warn of danger, others worked in shifts of 15 minutes, tearing at the mess of rocks, shale, and mine timbers.

In the meantime, word had been relayed through Cranbrook to Calgary and from there to eastern points. As was inevitable, the first reports were garbled and bordered on fantasy. Descriptions of the disaster ranged from a gigantic explosion in the mine to an earthquake, with over 100 bodies already found and upwards of 50 men imprisoned inside the mine.

The CPR acted promptly by sending a special train from Cranbrook to evacuate the stricken community. At the same time, the Dominion

Although upright, the Bansemer house was badly damaged and moved several feet. The men in front of it are standing on the rubble that buried the Clark house, killing Mrs. Alfred Clark and her five children. Her husband died also, killed when the slide demolished the mine tipple.

government dispatched William Pearce, chief inspector of surveys for the department of the interior, to take charge of the situation. While Inspector Davidson, NWMP officer in charge of the Pincher Creek sub-division, rode in with a sergeant and a constable to reinforce Constable Leard, a further force of 10 police under Inspector Douglas was rushed from Calgary. They were joined by another contingent of 25 men from Fort Macleod and Lethbridge. Their special train, loaded with correspondents from various newspapers, arrived at Frank at 4 a.m. on April 30. The *Calgary Herald*'s correspondent, impeccably attired, ensconced himself in a local hotel and began to send out reports without proper research. His articles were the source of much misinformation on the tragedy.

During the hectic day, business establishments closed, partly from respect and partly because no one was interested in shopping. The

The barroom of the Imperial Hotel in Frank was crowded with those who had viewed the calamity and wished to forget what they had seen.

hotel bars, by contrast, did a roaring business with those who had viewed the calamity and wished to forget as promptly as possible what they had seen.

In the little hospital and converted front room of Dr. Malcolmson's house, the doctor and his nurse, Miss Grassick, cared for the injured.

The NWMP, dispatched to assist the relief effort, camped near the Frank Slide. Nurse Grassick is one of the nurses standing in front of the log building.

They were pitifully few, for only a handful of residents who had been touched by the sea of rocks lived to remember the experience. Lester Johnson, bandaged to the armpits, revelled in the warmth. Jim Warrington, his upper thigh reset, struggled as he fought off the after-effects of ether. Mrs. Watkins, knowing her children were safe, fretted over the absence of her husband. No one dared tell her that he was among the trapped men in the mine.

The entombed miners

As Joe Chapman and his 19 men trudged up the spur line to the mine entrance that morning of April 29, 1903, they had no premonition of danger. It was true that strange things had been happening in the mine for the past seven months. Two-foot timbers set one night had been found splintered by the day crew, and upraises where the coal had been removed silently closed overnight. There had been a minor earthquake the year the mine opened, but this tremor had had no apparent ill effect. Two young miners had been killed in a gas explosion the previous October, but they apparently had been wearing the old-style open-flame lamps instead of the new safety lights.

The night crew left Tashigan at the mine tipple, where he operated the scales and coal-washing equipment. Then they entered the shaft via what had been a nearly vertical seam of coal about 30 feet above the river. The seam itself, varying in width from 13 to 15 feet, came from the direction of Goat Mountain, passed under the town of Frank and through Turtle Mountain in an almost north-south direction, paralleling the axis of the mountain itself. From the mouth of the mine, the drift rose sharply to a height of nearly 1,200 feet. Already the mine had been worked back some 5,000 feet. Because of the near-vertical nature of the main vein, mining was a simple operation. The coal was merely worked loose and allowed to fall down the incline to the main manway, where it was loaded on the mine cars and hauled by horse to the tipple on the outside.

At one time the mine had employed nearly 300 men, but in the winter of 1902 nearly one-third had been laid off. The mine was now operating only one shift, with a night crew for timbering and maintenance purposes.

As the miners penetrated the tunnel, they dropped off to their duties. Alex Grant and his driver took one of the five horses stationed at the entrance and began checking the trackage. Fred Farrington and Alfred Clark took other horses and started hauling out cars of coal left by the day shift. Timberman William Warrington set about his never-ending task of checking the mine timbers—testing and replacing damaged ones or setting up new ones.

As the night wore on, lamps glowed dimly in the tunnels and upraises. Some men worked alone, others in pairs. Toward 4:00 a.m.,

Clark and Farrington took loads of coal out to the mine tipple and sat down to eat their lunches with Tashigan.

Shortly afterward, Grant and his driver felt a shock, like a severe bump. Thinking it was a gas explosion and fearing it might be followed by afterdamp (deadly carbon monoxide gas), they raced toward the mine entrance. The tunnel around them was heaving and twisting, sending down small showers of rock and coal. When they reached the end of it, they found not daylight and safety, but a mass of shattered timbers and fallen rock. As they gazed in horror, they were joined by others running from the depths of the mine. One miner panicked at the sight of the blocked entrance and turned to flee. As he did so, he tripped and fell, wrenching his leg severely.

Further back in the manway, Joe Chapman felt the earth's shudder. Then a blast of hot air picked him up and slammed him against the tunnel wall. He recovered and ran for almost a mile along the crazily heaving tracks to the entrance.

Dan McKenzie had been working in an upraise some way back when a sudden blast of air, followed by a shower of coal, flung him against the side of the mine and gashed his head. Realizing that something unusual had happened, he ignored the wound to his head and raced down the manway.

At the blocked entrance, breathless from their frantic dashes for safety, 17 miners rested momentarily and then considered their position. One of them, who had worked the mine from its opening day and who knew intimately every inch of the timbering and tracks, examined the inside of their prison. He concluded that they were at least 300 feet from the outside. The news dismayed them, even though some of the more optimistic felt that they could not be more than 50 feet back. Leaving Warrington, whose leg had been severely squeezed by a collapsing crosscut, the rest made their way to the lower level, hoping to find the exit there still intact. They were dismayed to discover that it was already filling with water from the dammed Oldman River. Even as they watched, they saw the water rapidly backing up into the mine.

The mine was deathly quiet and the mountain had ceased to shudder as they made their way back to the entrance where Warrington and the other injured man waited. They now realized that their situation was grave. Cut off by rising water, sealed in by rock, they realized that if the air shafts had also been pinched, their supply would soon be fouled. It was possible also that the upheaval had loosened pockets of gas that would collect in the upper regions of the tunnels.

Maintaining their calm, they returned bravely to their original work places and collected their tools. Back at the entrance they began to try to battle their way through the shattered timbers and crumbled rocks.

While they were working, McKenzie and two others climbed 300 feet up ladders to the Nicholson Level, as the old workings were called. Gas was already collecting. More disastrously, their investigations revealed that the air shafts had been completely sealed. They returned to their comrades with this discouraging news.

The men working at the entrance were making little or no progress against the snarled mass of timber and rocks. Panic began to rise. At that point one man took charge. Some say it was Joe Chapman, the foreman, others say it was Dan McKenzie, while others believe it was Charlie Farrell. Whichever man it was knew where a seam of coal outcropped on the mountain some distance from the main portal. Believing that they were close enough to the surface to break free through the outcrop, the man convinced the others to start digging. They did not know how far they were from the surface or whether they might encounter an insurmountable barrier of rock. What they did know, however, was that their air was becoming more foul, more and more unable to keep them alive.

In the cramped shaft the men had to work in relays of two or three—slowly but steadily swinging their picks. Toward mid-afternoon, three of them returned to the main entrance to examine once again the rubble. The impossibility of escape that way was obvious.

Under the increasing strain and diminishing oxygen supply, some of the men became excited, others morose. In the beginning they had sung to boost their courage; now they were quiet, hoping to conserve the fast-faltering supply of air. Toward late afternoon they slumped, exhausted, against the mine wall. Only McKenzie and two others persevered.

Unexpectedly, McKenzie's pick drove into the open. A beam of brilliant sunlight blinded him and clean air bathed his face. The exhausted men, revived by the fresh air, renewed their fight for freedom. They quickly discovered that rocks still cascading down the mountainside prevented their escape via the new tunnel. Their morale now high, they started driving another shaft upward through 36 feet of coal and clay. Thirteen hours after the slide had sealed them in, they broke into daylight behind boulders that shielded them from the rockfalls.

McKenzie, the first man out, stared in astonishment. The slide fanned out from the base of Turtle Mountain like a giant's stubby-fingered hand of destruction on the valley floor. Small figures scrambled over the rocks, obviously searching. From a mass of broken timbers where the row of miners' cottages had stood, white smoke curled lazily into the late afternoon sky. Fifty yards below and to the left, a little knot of men battled the rubble blocking the mine entrance.

McKenzie called. They looked up, whooping with joy as they saw him. There was a scrambled rush across the treacherous slope, a grasping of hands, and exchange of news.

For John Watkins, whose anguished glance had revealed only a sea of

Fortunately for the miners, their tunnel emerged in front of a boulder, protecting them from rocks still hurtling down Turtle Mountain.

rocks and mud where his home should have been, the news was good. His three children had escaped and his wife was recovering in hospital.

For William Warrington, who had to be lifted on a plank because of his injured leg, there was tragic news. Only rock marked his temporary dwelling among the Jack pines. Even the possibility of a minor miracle was erased when he looked at the downcast faces of his rescuers. For him there was only the realization that his wife, four children, and friend, Alex Dixon, lay buried beneath the massive limestone grave.

The 17 men were hurried down the mountain and across the make-shift ferry. Since Farrington, Clark, and Tashigan were not among them, the tabulators added their names to the growing casualty list. A waiting wagon carried Warrington up the main street and across the flat to Dr. Malcolmson's hospital. While the other miners sought

The freed miners were escorted up Frank's main street as the slide loomed menacingly in the background. After reaching safety, the injured William Warrington (in the wagon) learned that his wife, their four children, and his friend were among the dead.

relatives and friends, some stopped at the hotel bar to wet throats still dry from fear.

Miracles are seldom wrought by one person. The escape of the miners entombed in Turtle Mountain was no exception. An ingenious and daring suggestion by one man pointed the way; the courage and strength of all 17 to follow that suggestion saved their lives.

Among the dead

All that day of April 29, massive rocks shook loose from the scarred crest and bounded down the sheer slope. Suddenly conscious that another enormous slice overhung the untouched part of the village, people fled their cottages, piling household goods into wagons or wheelbarrows. Whole families vacated the town and were loaded onto the special CPR train for transportation to Blairmore and points west.

A citizens' meeting had been convened by the president of the Board of Trade early in the morning. Search parties were sent into the ruins, but by nightfall only 12 bodies were recovered and removed to the temporary morgue in the schoolhouse. Most were so badly mutilated that identification had to be made through clothing or documents, or from the location where they were found.

For some it was a day of wonderment and awe. Ellen Thornley was horrified to realize that except for a whim, she and her brother would have been sleeping in the shoe shop that now lay beneath the rocks. Les Ferguson, who had parted company with Robert Watt a few hours before, searched unsuccessfully for his friend's body. Jack Leonard, returning from Pincher Creek after a successful hay-buying trip, gazed in disbelief on the rubble where his camp had been. He alone of the entire McVeigh and Poupore crew was alive.

There were the two Welsh miners and Alfred Dawe, who should have been on the CPR train, safely heading eastward and home—except for the mistake in their reservations. Dawe's terrier survived; they didn't.

Charles and Robert Chestnut also survived. The only reason, however, was that the cabin they were impatiently waiting to move into was occupied by the three delayed men.

The first hero of the tragedy was Sid Choquette, who had scrambled through the wilderness of rock to warn the approaching passenger train. An early rumour circulated that he had gone insane as a result of the awful scenes he had seen, but it was not so. Another reported that grateful passengers of the train presented him with a gold watch and the CPR guaranteed him a job for life. Again the rumours were untrue. Choquette and conductor Pettit were given cheques for $25 and letters of commendation. Later, Sid transferred to the Illinois Central Railroad and remained with that company until his retirement in the 1930s.

Early on the morning of April 30, the special train arrived from Fort Macleod, carrying 25 officers and men of the NWMP under the command of Inspector Primrose. Doctors Kennedy and Edwards of Fort Macleod accompanied the train with their nurses, but there was little they could do. The need for doctors and nurses was not acute, since most of those overtaken by the flood of limestone had been killed instantly and the survivors had already received medical attention from Dr. Malcolmson and Nurse Grassick. Kennedy and Edwards returned almost at once to their own practices.

The following day, Premier Haultain arrived. He immediately held a meeting with the Board of Trade. As a result, a party of engineers and mountain experts were dispatched to the top of Turtle Mountain to determine what danger might remain.

In the meantime, 130 men working for Breckenridge and Lund who had been scheduled to begin improving the grade of the CPR line near Frank were brought from Morrissey and put to work clearing the river to prevent further serious flooding. Others were organized into crews to build a road around the north end of the slide. More men joined them, until the work crew numbered 1,000 strong.

As rock had ceased falling by the morning of May 1, many townspeople began returning to their homes. Plans were laid by J.S. McCarthy, acting mine superintendent, to reopen the mine and explore the full extent of the damage. One of the employees succeeded in entering the mine through the tunnel excavated by the trapped miners and reported that the main tunnel was not severely damaged. He estimated damage at about $75,000.

When the exploratory party returned from the summit of Turtle Mountain, their report was both reassuring and disturbing. Along the section overlooking Frank, they had found huge fissures, some over 150 feet deep, but had not detected evidence of another potential slide.

As a result Premier Haultain, after assuring himself that there was no destitution among the survivors, began the slow, two-hour climb over the slide to his special train.

At the east edge of the rocks he was met by A. McHenry, the CPR's chief engineer, who had spent the day watching the mountaintop through binoculars. He was convinced that it was shifting toward the edge. At any moment, he expected more gigantic slices to plunge down on the remainder of the town.

At this news, Haultain and his party at once returned and held a second meeting with the Board of Trade and Inspector Primrose. They decided to evacuate Frank immediately. The injured were put aboard special cars and transported half a mile west to the NWMP barracks, which became a temporary hospital. By nightfall Frank was deserted, displaced citizens waiting with dread for news that a new fall had obliterated their homes and businesses.

A "dead-line" was drawn at Frank's west end and patrolled night and day by the police. No one was permitted to enter the area at night and during the day only those having legitimate business were allowed through. Inside Frank, the police maintained a rigid patrol. As a result, not a single case of looting occurred while the town was empty.

One of the few people permitted through the police cordon was Harry J. Matheson, editor of the *Frank Sentinel*. Matheson, displaying true journalistic spirit, rolled his press despite the potential peril of another slide. He wrote:

"The conduct of our citizens when the disaster occurred here on Wednesday was praiseworthy in the extreme ..." But he also noted: "The arrival of the police was very timely as already vicious and cowardly elements, of which there are some in every community, had early taken to the bottle and drunken rowdies were strongly in evidence on our streets."

The edition appeared on time.

To Matheson fell the unhappy task of setting in print the list of casualties—many of whom he had known. He listed 76, but the total has since grown to 81. No one knows for certain how many men were in the construction camp that night, since all records were buried; no one knows how many, like Robert Watt, went back to visit or sleep in the temporary shacks and tents in the eastern flats. Rumour persists that about 50 men were camped on the recreation ground, now buried under rock and mud. While many of the casualties were listed as dead because of their continued absence, the bulk of evidence was circumstantial. No one will ever know how many really died in the battering wind, pulverizing rocks, suffocating dust, or rising water. Only 12 bodies were recovered.

While in later years many persons claimed to be survivors because they had been resident in Frank at the time, technically only those who had been "in the rocks" were true claimants to the honour. Others, like Lillian Clark, Jack Leonard, or Ellen and John Thornley, were survivors only in the sense that fate had dictated their presence elsewhere.

The real survivors were few: Mrs. John Watkins and her three children; Sam and Lucy Ennis and their four children; James Warrington; Lester Johnson; the three Leitch girls; and Annie Bansemer with her seven children. In all, 23 fortunate people.

To these must be added the 17 miners, but the inadequacy of records has drawn a curtain over some of them. Those known include Joseph Chapman, Dan McKenzie, Evan Jones, William Warrington, Alex W. Grant, "Shorty" Dawson, Alex McPhail, John Watkins, Charles Farrell, and Charles Elick. There were seven others whose courage had enabled them to survive.

The aftermath

For nine days a careful watch was kept on the shoulder of Turtle Mountain directly above Frank. On May 10, Premier Haultain returned for a meeting with CPR engineer McHenry. After an encouraging report that there seemed to be no movement, Haultain advised the residents they were free to return to their homes.

Despite this reassuring news, there was no stampede back to Frank. Merchants and hotel keepers reopened their businesses, but 10 days later only two houses had been reoccupied. Since the mine was still closed, however, there was no great incentive for people to leave the assured safety of Blairmore. Even the hotels had few guests.

On Sunday, May 24, a large group of sightseers flocked from surrounding towns to view the damage. Their curiosity was interrupted when 100 pounds of dynamite being thawed by the railway builders exploded. A panicky crowd raced for shelter. Fortunately, no one was injured.

On May 30, workers at the mine reported they had made an opening to the old workings. As they explored the manways they found, to their amazement, Charlie, one of the mine horses. He had survived both the cave-ins and days of starvation. The other horses, stabled near the mine entrance while their drivers had lunch, had both been killed. Charlie had survived by drinking seepage water, sucking his harness for salt, and gnawing wood from the coal cars and timbers. He was unable to survive the welcome of his rescuers, however, for shortly after, he succumbed to an overdose of brandy and oats.

When the explorations revealed that the main workings were intact for some 5,000 feet, Samuel Gebo, one of the partners in the mine, announced that it would be reopened immediately. But hard luck prevailed. In 1905 two serious fires drove the miners out, while seepage from the lake, which had been formed by the rock slide, made operations very difficult. To avoid this seepage a new shaft-type mine was started some distance back from the original workings.

In 1908, H.L. Frank would die, confined in his last months to a private sanatorium, his mind broken, it is said, by memories of his ill-fated mining venture. Subsequently, the mine was sold.

Following the slide, the Dominion government sent R.G. McConnell and R.W. Brock of the Geological Survey of Canada to investigate. By early June 1903 their report was completed and noted, in part:

"The management state that the mine was in first class condition before the catastrophe, that the walls were solid, that there were no more movements or breaking away of the hanging wall than is usual in coal mines, and that the timbers were not under undue strain. Mr. Chestnut, a miner, states that slight movements were noticeable during the last seven months. These were particularly liable to occur between one and three in the morning. He describes them as like the starting and shuddering of a ship struck by a wave. Mr. Chapman (the foreman) also stated that these shocks were most frequent between the hours of one and three in the morning. These

Charlie, one of the mine horses, amazingly survived several weeks in the black tunnel. Sadly, a warm welcome of brandy and oats from his rescuers killed him.

tremors were somewhat alarming to the miners, and some are said to have left the mine on account of them.

"It is also reported that lately the coal has been mined with unusual ease, often running itself, so that the miners were taken off contract work and put upon day work. Rock from the hanging wall is said to have been falling in and mixing with the coal, so that men had to be employed in picking it out when the cars were dumped.

"Cyrus Morris, formerly underground superintendent, stated that for the last seven months, there had been a general squeeze in the ground between 3,500 and 5,000 feet in the tunnel. The coal could be kept up only with difficulty. It was broken and would mine itself."

On the final reason for the slide, the report stated:

"The snapping of the last threads supporting the peak which broke away, that is the final cause of the slide, was in all probability due to the temperature conditions during and preceding the morning of April 29.

"The night of the slide was excessively cold. The miners say that it was colder than any night during the winter. Those outside state that the temperature was down to zero. The day before and the preceding days had been very hot, so that the fissures in the mountain must have been filled with water, on which the frost would act with powerful effect.

"The rock slide cannot, therefore, be considered as due to a single cause, but rather, like so many phenomena in nature, to a combination of causes, cumulative in their effects. The chief of these were the structure and condition of the mountain, aided by exceptional atmospheric and other natural conditions, and also, possibly, by slight readjustments in the lower strata attendant on mining operations."

Frank's problems did not end when the massive slide stabilized, for the community still lived under the shadow of death. As the report noted:

"The fractured zone surrounding the old break is bound sooner or later to fall away, but whether it falls gradually in small comparatively harmless blocks, or in large destructive masses depends upon future conditions, which cannot be foretold. The shattered mass between the north and south peaks does not menace the town, as the falling material will travel over the former slide. Moreover, the fracturing is so complete, that it is rapidly falling in individual blocks, which, though large, are yet not large enough for their momentum to carry them to the base of the mountain …

"That part of the north peak lying east of the fissure, 150 feet from the face, along which it slipped during our observations, threatens the mouth of the main tunnel of the mine, since, if it falls in one block, it will certainly reach the base of the mountain near the edge of the former slide. More danger to the town is apprehended from the fissures that exist behind and further to the west of the north peak. These fissures are narrow, but are wide enough to admit water, and the pressure of the rock above may keep them closed until the undermining action of the water, or some other cause, liberates the superincumbent mass and a slide results. The safety of the town depends upon the stability of the shoulder protruding eastward from the north peak ... The breaking away of the central portion of the mountain, which is going on continuously, is also tending to weaken this northern shoulder. If the town is to remain inhabited in its present position, these northern fissures must be closely watched. They are not likely to slip or extend suddenly (although, as stated above, there is always some liability of their doing so), and for this reason the upper portion of the town is not considered to be in any great immediate danger. If, however, any signs of slipping along the fissures some distance back from the north peak are detected, the town ought to at once be evacuated.

"The town of Frank might exist on its present site uninjured for ages, but there will always be a possibility of a second destructive slide. The fact that the north shoulder withstood the shock of the first slide and was so solid that a snow cornice over its face was not broken down, is no proof that it is too solid to fall. A succession of seasons with unusually heavy precipitations and rapid changes of temperature, a slight earthquake shock, which is by no means an impossibility, or the closing of the chambers in the mine after the coal has been drawn, perhaps long after the inhabitants have lost all dread of the mountain, may snap the supports which retain this mass in place and start it on a career of destruction.

"Since this possibility must always overhang the town it certainly seems in the interests of safety that it be moved a short distance up the valley, beyond the reach of danger."

Additional examinations during forthcoming years reinforced the conclusions of the original report, especially since several large fissures opened in the section overlooking Frank. In 1911 the Dominion government appointed a commission of two geologists and an engineer to investigate further and recommend a policy. The commission noted that the cracks in the rocks near the summit were widening and also agreed that another slide could happen. While they felt that the mining company could not be blamed for the first slide, they could be held responsible if a second occurred. They recommended that the part of Frank under the north peak be moved to a safer location, joining the part of Frank already north of the CPR tracks. As a consequence, the Dominion government ordered the move. Some buildings also moved to Blairmore, and other parts of the pass or beyond.

While the shift in location had a disruptive effect, it did not cause the death of the once-flourishing community. The coal mine was responsible. It closed in 1917, not because company officials feared that it might cause a second rockfall, but because it was no longer competitive. What remained of Frank was torn down, moved, or fell into decay.

By then the old stagecoach road through the north end of the slide had been replaced by another that traversed the slide at the base of Turtle Mountain. A twisting route through the boulders, it is still used, emerging at the east end near abandoned lime kilns. Not far from the kilns, somewhere under the rocks, lie James Graham's ranch house and its six occupants. The western end is close to where the row of miners' houses stood that tragic night of April 29, 1903.

In 1922, while widening the west end, workmen uncovered skeletons and parts of a cradle. Old-timers believed they were the remains of the Clark family. The bones and other grim mementoes were buried where they were found: a memorial now identifies the location. In 1949, while a steam shovel was loading CPR trains with ballast rock, some of the original trackage and a case of footwear that might have come from Thornley's shoe store were uncovered. In the early 1930s, a new highway was built north of the railway line, a route that today is part of Highway Number 3, linking southern Alberta and B.C. through the Crowsnest Pass.

Over the years, solid reminders of the devastation from that epic 90 seconds have gradually disappeared. Included were the wheels of the coal car which Choquette and his companions were spotting as the slide began. No one bothered to preserve them and they were melted in a reduction furnace.

What has not disappeared, however, are the myths that arose even before the last unstable rocks crashed downward. The tragedy of the slide itself, its 69 or more bodies still entombed, the self-rescue of the trapped miners, and the narrow escapes of many residents is dramatic enough without any elaboration. Nevertheless, there were those who tried to change the truth or capitalize on it.

For instance, despite the fact that 23 people came out of the rocks and another 17 from the mine, and despite the fact that nine-tenths of the town's population was unscathed, unscrupulous persons were able to pass themselves off during the summers of 1903 and 1904 in the eastern United States as the "sole survivor." The Union Bank stood for eight more years on its original foundations, but hardly had it been torn down in 1911 than a rumour started that it had been buried, together with $500,000 in American silver dollars.

The miraculous escape of baby Marion Leitch, who was flung from her shattered home, has also been distorted many times. Romanticists and pseudo-historians created the myth of "Frankie Slide" and had her found everywhere from on a rock to dead in her mother's arms. She was also credited with being the only survivor, although her two sisters and a score of other citizens also survived. When Marion Leitch grew up she married Lawrence McPhail and lived until 1977.

Today, the cascade of death that ruptured from Turtle Mountain still lies like an enormous scar across the valley of the Crowsnest Pass. To tens of thousands of motorists who pause at the viewpoint each year, it is a reminder of 90 seconds of wind, rock, and dust—an awesome tombstone where lie at least 81 people.

A memorial plaque serves as a headstone for those bodies still entombed beneath the rocks.

In Memoriam

Names and variations of names of victims, according to three sources from that time in history:

Charles Ackroyd and wife

Joe Britton (Brighton?)

Alfred Clark, Millie Clark, children: Charles, Albert, Alfred, Ellen, Gertrude

J.W. Clark (Clarke?)

Ben Cunes, wife, two children

Alfred "Jack" Dawe (Dawes?) and two friends from Wales

Thomas Delap

Alex Dixon

Fred Farrington

T. (D?) Foster

Alex Graham and wife

James Graham, wife, two sons

Andrew Grissack Jr.

J. (John?) Gustavus

Two Johnson (Johnstone?) brothers

E. (Ed?) Kruss

Alexander Leitch, Rosemary Leitch, sons: John, Wilfred, Allen, Athol

G. (George?) Lemosike

Thomas R. Lock (Locke?)

M. Madigan

John McVeigh

Francis Rochette

J.J. Scott

J. Siotta

Alexander Tashigan

James Vandusen, wife, two children

F. Vocken (Vochen?)

Mrs. William Warrington, four children

Robert Watt

George Williams, wife, four children (three?)

D. Yonack

At least six unknown men

Four Finlanders, names unknown

Barney Surris

B. Yeskes

Dave Johnson

Jacob Tourni

Jacob Sorri

HILLCREST
MINE DISASTER

Frank Anderson

EDITOR'S INTRODUCTION

As I now descend into the dark bowels of the earth, I beseech thee, sweet Barbara, that I be kept safe from harm, for it liketh me not that I rush unbidden into God's presence. So reads a prayer to Saint Barbara, patron saint of miners. Coal mining has always been an occupation fraught with peril. The Crowsnest Pass coal miner of the early 20th century tended to be a tougher breed of man with large, muscled hands and nerves of steel. Enduring relentless risk, coal miners came face to face with their mortality every day and made peace with it. Those who had never been a miner wondered how these steadfast souls could descend into the very heart of danger time after time. But the coal miners would tell them that once coal was in the blood, there was no way out. Some coal miners developed rituals and beliefs that allowed them to cope. But their precautions could not keep them safe always.

The first explosion on the Alberta side of the Crowsnest Pass occurred in the International mine at Coleman, about three miles west of Blairmore, on April 3, 1907. All those underground survived the blast itself, but three miners died from the afterdamp. Coleman's second explosion was at the McGillivray mine in 1926. Ten miners died. The blast occurred on the night shift, when few men were working. Had it occurred on the day shift, the death toll could have been 20 to 30 times higher. As it was, the mine caught fire and had to be flooded. It was months before grieving relatives could retrieve and bury their sons, husbands, and fathers.

Three miles east of Blairmore another mining community, Bellevue, had its first—and only—disaster on December 9, 1910. Thirty miners and one rescuer died in an explosion south of the town. Residents were horror-stricken at the disaster, little knowing it would be dreadfully overshadowed less than four years later.

On the morning of June 19, 1914, men left their homes at Bellevue's neighbouring community of Hillcrest and climbed to their awaiting fate. The Hillcrest mine was considered the safest mine in the area, having operated for nine years with no serious accidents. Tragically, at 9:30

Coal miners with their tools and lanterns are shown ready to descend into the mine at Hillcrest, Alberta, 1912.

that Friday morning something triggered a methane gas fire. It skipped along the roof of the mine tunnel until it encountered a pocket of coal dust. There was a massive series of explosions, followed by killing afterdamp. Of the 235 miners who went underground that morning, 189 died in Canada's worst mine disaster. Virtually every family in Hillcrest was affected. Some 130 women were left without a husband and 400 children without a father. The dead men were buried in three graves, the largest 200 feet long and containing 150 bodies in two rows.

The mine reopened and operated free of major accidents until September 19, 1926. That afternoon, some 150 men were making final preparations to start their night shift. In the mine were only two men—fireboss Frank Lote and Fred Jones, who was attending the pumping system. There was a sudden thunderous explosion. Rescuers found both men dead, and there was evidence that the blast was more devastating than the one in 1914 that took 189 lives. Had it occurred two hours later, 150 men would have been in the tunnels.

The number of disasters has almost been equalled on the B.C. side of the Crowsnest Pass. At the now-abandoned community of Crowsnest, near the B.C.–Alberta border, there is a cemetery containing some 30 graves. They are believed to be those of railway construction workers who died in 1898 of typhoid fever.

The worst mine disaster in the B.C. portion of the Crowsnest Pass was on May 22, 1902, at Coal Creek—today called Fernie. That day an explosion in No. 2 mine took 128 lives. It still ranks with the greatest coal-mine catastrophes in Canada.

Further tragedies awaited the Coal Creek mine. In a 1917 explosion, another 34 miners died; in 1928 six more were killed, and in 1935 an additional three died in a "bump," or underground movement of the earth. In all, the mine took over 160 lives.

Other communities wracked by fires and explosions were Michel and Natal, about halfway through the pass. In 1904 seven men died in an explosion that set Michel on fire and destroyed half of it. While the cause was never ascertained, a careless workman was believed to be responsible.

On August 8, 1916, a mysterious blast occurred in No. 3 mine near the eastern entrance to Natal. The blast occurred during a thunderstorm and killed 12 men. No satisfactory reason was uncovered. Lightning was considered a possible cause, but the theory was rejected.

At Michel on July 15, 1938, an explosion rocked No. 3 mine, also during a thunderstorm. The mine was idle that day, a lucky circumstance for those on the regular shift. Unfortunately, of five maintenance men inside, only two survived. This time the cause was unmistakable. Lightning had struck the mine rails and caused the killer explosion deep inside the tunnel. The steel rails were grounded and another potential hazard was defused, although at least 15 men had died before the deadly hazard was identified.

The last in the Crowsnest Pass mine disasters that have killed more than 500 miners occurred at Michel on April 3, 1967. The afternoon shift of 32 men entered Balmer North mine, operated by Crow's Nest Industries Limited. A few minutes later an explosion—or series of

Motor cars and crew gathered at the entrance to No. 2 mine at Coal Creek, 1902, shortly before the explosion of May 22 that killed 128 miners. Of these men and boys, only four would survive.

explosions—turned the tunnels into a tomb. Fifteen miners died—nearly 50 percent of those who had gone underground a few minutes before.

What follows is Frank Anderson's gripping account of the horrific Hillcrest mine disaster.

Break of dawn

The sun peeked over the horizon, glanced at the scarred face of Turtle Mountain, scanned the crags and peaks of the Livingstone Range and then, as if satisfied, leaped hot and red into the June morning sky. It sent its rays glimmering over the mining communities of Burmis, Leitch Collieries, Maple Leaf, and Bellevue, into the peaceful flats between Bellevue and Hillcrest, over the ghostly ruins of the Frank Slide, and on through the gap between Goat and Turtle mountains. It lit the tipple of Hillcrest Collieries, then followed the mine tracks around the gently sweeping mountainside until it found the concrete mine buildings nestling in the valley between Hillcrest and Turtle mountains. Here it caught the eyes of William Adkin, fireboss, as he stepped from the mouth of Mine No. 1, forcing him to squint against the brilliance of the new day dawning in the Crowsnest Pass.

It was 6:20 a.m., June 19, 1914. Adkin had just completed an inspection of the mine in preparation for the morning shift due to arrive at 7:00 a.m. As part of his responsibility, he posted a notice on the bulletin board in the lamphouse. It advised that he had found pockets of gas in certain sections of the mine, some cave-ins and rockfall in other parts. That done, he checked with timekeeper Robert Hood and went off duty.

The Hillcrest mine was considered the safest and best-run operation in the Crowsnest Pass. Its coal had been discovered in 1900 by Charles Plummer Hill, a United States customs officer who spent his free time scouring the mountains for minerals. Hill had been in no hurry to develop the property and it was January 1905 before serious mining started.

In 1909 Hill sold the mines, originally known as the Hillcrest Coal and Coke Company, to a group of Montreal developers. They reorganized the project under the name of Hillcrest Collieries Limited and invested large sums of money to enlarge and modernize the operation.

Hill's original Mine No. 1 entered the mountain through a rock tunnel some 200 feet long, then dipped down Slant No. 1 for another 1,200 feet. From here radiated an intricate series of tunnels and passageways. Later, a second mine was opened about 500 feet to the south and it was known as Mine No. 2. By June 1914 this mine descended gently into the side of the mountain, along Slant No. 2 to a distance of 2,400 feet. These workings were joined to Slant No. 1 by two main intersecting tunnels, Level 1 and Level 2 South. Again, a complicated pattern of tunnels ran from them to give access to the coal seams.

The third major section of the mine was opened in 1912. Known as Level 1 North, it swept in a huge semicircle from a point 900 feet down Slant No. 2. Unlike the other two major workings, there was only one entrance to this part of the mine.

By June 1914, Hillcrest Collieries had 377 men on the payroll. Most of them lived in Hillcrest, although some came from the neighbouring village of Bellevue and from houses and cottages scattered along the valley floor. The majority were married, earning an average of $125 a month, and, despite periodic layoffs, enjoying a high standard of living.

Because of overproduction, the mine was closed June 17-18 and scheduled to reopen on June 19. Accordingly, on the 18th, a pit committee of Frank Pearsons, president of the Miners' Union, with miners George Pounder and James Gurtson, toured the three major workings. They found them

The coal-mining town of Hillcrest, Alberta, in 1914, with Frank Slide rubble visible at upper left.

in satisfactory condition for resumption of work on Friday morning, June 19.

Fireboss Daniel Briscoe went on duty at 3:00 p.m. One of his duties was to inspect the mine for accumulations of coal dust, gas, or any other dangerous condition. Briscoe found gas in several sections of the mine and posted warning signs, but he reported that the ventilation was good and that there was plenty of moisture. Because of the highly explosive nature of coal dust, a vital safety factor was adequate moisture to dampen the dust and reduce the danger of explosion. At 11 o'clock that evening, he was relieved by fireboss William Adkin who, during his night shift, checked on the presence of gas, coal dust, and moisture,

then remained until the morning shift came on duty at 7:00 a.m.

One man who missed the morning shift was William Dodd, 63, the oldest miner employed by Hillcrest Collieries. An old-timer in the pass, he had worked in almost every mine from Lethbridge to Fernie in British Columbia. Old Bill was damned if he was going to start work on a Friday. He stayed home—a decision that probably saved his life.

Dan Cullinen was employed on the afternoon shift. But when his friend, J.D. "Knicky Knack" Redmonson, developed a pain in his side, Cullinen took his place on the morning crew. As a consequence, Redmonson would live; his friend, die.

Tom Corkill, who had already survived a terrible blast in the Kenmore mines, went to work that morning with a feeling of nostalgia. This was to be his last shift in the Hillcrest workings. He had bought a homestead in the Lethbridge area and would be leaving for it the next day.

Thomas Dugdale of Bellevue awoke at 6:00 a.m. to hear three of his brothers stirring in the house. The oldest of five Dugdale boys, Tom had arrived in Canada from Scotland and found work in the Bellevue mines. Shortly after he had started, an explosion snuffed out the lives of 30 of his fellow miners. Tom had been off duty that day.

Following the death of their father, Tom's brothers—John, Robert, Andrew, and Peter, with their mother—joined him in Canada. All five brothers eventually started working for Hillcrest Collieries. Today, Robert, Andrew, and John, who was the assistant timekeeper on the morning shift, were preparing for work. Thomas, glad that he and Peter were on the afternoon shift, went back to sleep.

Meanwhile the buckers, the timber packers, the bratticemen, and others who worked the underground tunnels left their homes to rendezvous at the mine tipple and climb the road leading to the mine buildings. One who did not climb was Steve Belopotosky, a regular on the early shift. As a favour to a friend whose wife was arriving from Britain that afternoon, he, too, had traded shifts.

Rod Wallis and his brother-in-law, William Neath, walked mechanically up the road. Tired of mining, they looked forward to Monday when they would be headed for their homes in Nova Scotia, where they intended to resume farming. Fate had decreed, however, that neither would ever again see their home province.

By 6:45 a.m. the roadway was alive with some 250 men climbing toward a rendezvous with fate. About halfway up they lost sight of Hillcrest as the road entered the little valley that nestled between Hillcrest and Turtle mountains.

Turtle Mountain had special significance for one man who climbed that morning. Charles Elick had been one of 20 men on night duty at the Frank mine on the morning of April 29, 1903, when 90 million tons of rock broke from the face of Turtle Mountain and swept down the slope. Three miners had been killed at the mine tipple while Elick and 16 companions were trapped inside the mine. With the mine entrance blocked off, the ventilation shafts destroyed, and deadly gas filtering through the workings, Elick and his mates had fought panic and exhaustion and dug for 13 hours through a narrow seam of coal to the surface. This day Charles Elick was not to be so fortunate.

The Hillcrest Collieries buildings were on two levels. The roadway ended on a lower level, which contained the concrete wash house and the power house. Twenty feet above this level was the mine yard, which contained a machine repair shop, a small shelter for horses, a combined office and supply building, and the lamphouse. The entrances to both mines were on this level, with a hoist house at the mouth of each mine. The mine railroad, along which coal cars were hauled to the tipple around the corner of the mountain, used this level as a roadbed.

As the men reached the lower level, those who worked outside the mines broke ranks and went to their places of work, while 235 men filed into the lamphouse. Here they picked up their equipment, their lamps, and two brass tags with each man's number stamped upon them. From the lamphouse they crossed to the timekeeper's office, where they checked in with Robert Hood, the methodical timekeeper who had the reputation of never having cheated a miner, or let one slip an unworked hour past him.

The majority of the men who tramped through the timekeeper's office at 7:00 a.m. were in their late 20s or early 30s, most related by blood or marriage. The oldest was Robert Muir, 54; the youngest, Alex Petrie, 17. Alex and his two brothers, James and Robert, lived with their widowed mother in Hillcrest, where she operated a café with her two daughters.

One of the men, John B. McKinnon, was known as the "Samson of the Pass." He stood 6 feet 4 inches, weighed 215 pounds, and was reputed to be the strongest miner in western Canada. A week previously at Frank, he had picked up a 480-pound piece of railway track and hoisted it over his head for the amusement of his friends.

As they passed through the timekeeper's office, each man left one brass identification check with Robert Hood, who put it up on the checkboard and kept the second. This way any man still in the mine could be identified if their tag was on the board. Because fireboss William Adkin had reported gas in several tunnels, mine superintendent James S. Quigley entered first. With him was a team of bratticemen—specialists whose job was to maintain the system of screens that controlled the flow of air through the mines.

Air for the shafts was drawn in by a huge steam-driven fan and forced into Level 1 North. Inside the mine, the direction of flow was controlled by a series of brattices, screens made of heavy canvas coated with tar, to ventilate those areas where men were working or in which undue amounts of gas had collected. From Level 1 North, the air flowed northward in controlled streams and was drawn out by a second giant fan near the entrance to Mine No. 1. Since the miners carried no oxygen, their survival depended upon the smooth functioning of these two fans. When gas was reported at any sector, the bratticemen redirected the airflow to channel any accumulated gas back into the main air stream to dilute it.

Quigley and his men were followed within 15 minutes by the rest of the miners. Most entered through the rock tunnel and dispersed to their various places by descending Slant No. 1. About 50 men entered the second mine, the bulk of them proceeding into Level 1 North.

Before entering the mine, Sam Charlton, the fireboss who relieved Adkin, stopped at the powder house to pick up a supply of blasting powder and material from John Dugdale, popularly known as "Jock, the powder monkey." After signing for the powder, Charlton went into Mine No. 1. As he worked toward Old Level 1, he set off several charges.

In other parts of the mine, men moved through the inky blackness, paths illuminated only by their Wolf safety lamps. Like ants in a giant anthill, they moved surely and expertly to their jobs, each knowing that in many instances his life and others depended on the quality of his workmanship. Some repaired and checked the mine tracks, some laid new rails, and some installed new supporting timbers. Bratticemen constantly checked the flow of air, mechanics and electricians moved from electric engines to pumps, and carpenters hammered away in

Hillcrest Mine, 1914

Scale: approx 1/4 inch = 100 feet

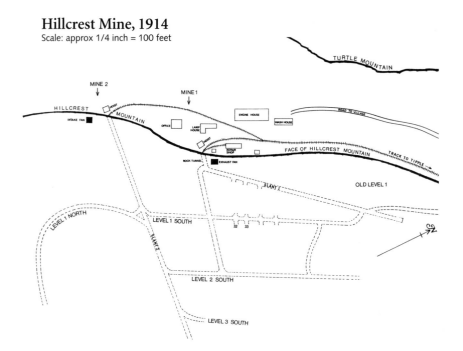

While this map was copied from the original blueprint, only the main passageways are indicated. In reality, intricate patterns of tunnels and slopes interlaced the whole area from Slant No. 2 northward and on both sides of Level 1 North. Evidence points to funnel 33 near the centre of the drawing as the point of explosion.

the tomb-like darkness. Miners dug the coal, then buckers shoved it through the chutes into mine cars. The cars were hauled by horses along the levels to the main slants. The mine cars were then hooked onto a continuous cable system and drawn to the surface by the hoists just outside the mine entrances.

At these entrances, young men known as "rope-riders" unhooked the cars and shunted them onto the tracks outside. That morning Charles Ironmonger was the rope-rider at Mine 1, while Fred Kurigatz performed the same function at the other mine.

At 8:00 a.m. fireboss John Ironmonger checked in at the timekeeper's office. He picked up a supply of blasting powder from Jock, then stopped for a brief chat with his son, Charles, before going down into Level 1 North. Another of his sons, Sam, was on duty as a timber-packer boss. After checking the dust content, moisture level, and air circulation, Ironmonger set off five charges to blast more coal face open for the miners.

At 9:00 a.m. eight more miners passed through the lamphouse, collected their lamps and brass checks, and went into the timekeeper's office. Hood passed six of them, but refused to let two into the mine when he detected the smell of liquor. Although Hood weighed only 140 pounds, there was no argument from the miners. They left the brass checks on his counter and returned their equipment to the lamphouse. That done, they wended their way back to the Miners' Hall to supplement their liquid intake. Without thinking, Hood picked up the two checks and hung them on the board with the others.

Down in the village, eight-year-old Jonathan Penn heard the school bell and raced out of the house. Without a glance toward the mine, where his father and older brother worked, he ran across the flats and got into his desk by the window in time to escape the teacher's questioning eye.

At the Petrie Café, two men lingered over cups of coffee before walking over to the Miners' Hall for some stiffer refreshment. Charles Elick's wife, expecting their child, began her daily round of house chores. Three men at the Miners' Hall, who should have been at work, contemplated the amber fluid in their glasses and philosophically pondered the meaning of wet circles on the tabletop. At the same time, James Quigley's wife was walking two younger children to their new house, which was completed the week before.

Alex May, an outside engineer whose duty it was to inspect and maintain the two giant fans that blew in and exhausted the air in the workings, finished his inspection of the intake fan and crossed over to inspect the second.

Deep in Old Level 1, fireboss Sam Charlton, married barely a month, prepared two charges of powder in a coalface at tunnel 32. Normally, he would have uncoiled the firing cable, which he carried wound around his leg, taken the battery from his pocket, connected them, and set off the explosion with a firing key. For some reason, he hesitated.

Thomas Bardsley, a miner in Level 1 South, raised his pick to a slab of coal. The pick never fell.

Holocaust

In that instant, somewhere in the miles of narrow, dark tunnels, a lamp flared, or a spark flew, or an electric cable shorted. The ever-present gas that hugged the tunnel roofs caught fire and skipped with lightning speed to a pocket of coal dust. In a fraction of a second, there was a massive explosion that triggered a second—and possibly a third—earth-shuddering blast.

Thomas Bardsley was transfixed in death by the violence of the explosion that cracked through the passages. His pick still clutched in upraised hands, his shirt collar blown 40 feet away, he stared with lifeless eyes at a seam of coal.

Alex May, working at the mouth of Mine No. 1, was dropped to his knees by the blast. When he looked back at the fan he had just inspected, he saw an ominous brown cloud of smoke rising from the ventilation shaft. The fan was motionless.

General manager John Brown, who had just seen the roof of a hoist house crumple from the impact of an invisible fist, ran toward the mine entrance. Jock Dugdale raced out of his powder room: "Mr. Brown, there's a fire in the mine!"

"My God! It's worse than that," Brown replied. "Get an electrician, quick."

As Dugdale raced for an electrician, outside workers converged on the mine entrance.

In the village school, Jonathan Penn lost track of what the teacher was saying. He watched instead a plume of brown smoke climb slowly into the morning sky. Then he saw people flooding from their houses and running toward the mine. There was no more school that day.

The first man found by the outside workers was Charles Ironmonger, the rope-rider at Mine No. 1. The explosion, which raced up the main tunnels from deep in the mine, had picked him up and hurled him 60 feet against the hoist house, at the same time blowing down the eight-inch thick concrete wall. Although Ironmonger was still alive, he was scarcely breathing. They placed him on a wagon and rushed him to the little village hospital, but he died a few moments later. He was the first known casualty.

Others, heedless of the danger of another blast, raced to No. 1, only to find that the blast had jammed the mouth with fallen rock, wrecked

The explosion raced up the main tunnels from deep in the mine and blew down the eight-inch thick concrete wall of this hoist house, 60 feet from the mine entrance.

mine cars, and smashed timbers. There was no way in—or out—of the rock tunnel.

At the entrance to Mine No. 2, the destruction was repeated. The other rope-rider, Fred Kurigatz, was killed instantly after being thrown against the hoist house. Here the blast had lifted the roof from the building and caved in the concrete wall facing the mine. By some miracle, the hoist engine was still operable and the cable undamaged.

Two men rushed into the mouth of No. 2, but were driven out by gas and smoke, one of them barely making it to safety. Another, searching for his brother, rushed in and out several times but was driven back. He had to abandon his search.

Meanwhile, the electrician had managed to restart the fan above Mine No. 1 and reverse the wiring so that it began to draw fresh air into the mine. Since the fan at Mine No. 2 was still functioning, it meant that both fans were bringing air into the corridors. Brown's quick action saved many lives among the miners who had survived the explosion but were now trapped in the gas-filled mine.

The explosions—one survivor reported hearing three separate blasts which seemed to come so close together that they were one—had burned the oxygen out of the air. Left now was deadly carbon dioxide, called "blackdamp" and carbon monoxide, called "afterdamp" by the miners. Air containing only 13 percent carbon dioxide is sufficient to cause unconsciousness and death after prolonged exposure. Following the gigantic explosion, it was estimated that nearly 50 percent of the remaining air was composed of carbon dioxide. Carbon monoxide kills even more quickly.

The time of the explosions was placed at 9:30 a.m. A few minutes later, three men—George Wild, Arthur Crowther, and Antonio Stella—staggered from the mouth of Mine No. 2. They had been working only a short distance inside the entrance and had miraculously escaped the deadly blast that swept up Slant No. 2.

By then a call for help had been sent to Blairmore, where a government rescue car with full equipment was stationed. In the meantime the few men left on the surface worked frantically to clear the wreckage around the entrance to Mine No. 2. As there was no hope of clearing Mine No. 1, they concentrated on putting the second hoist into operation. With each passing minute, more and more white-faced men arrived from the village.

At Burmis Mines, about two and a half miles from Hillcrest, word of the disaster quickly reached the Royal NWMP, and corporals Frederick John Mead and Arthur Grant, with Constable William Hancock, raced to the scene on horseback.

The police arrived to find women and children swarming around the mine. "People were frantically trying to push through to see if their loved ones were anywhere in sight," said Constable Hancock later. "Having heard the explosion, and knowing their men had already gone to work, and would be in the mine, they were still hopeful that some miracle may have spared them."

Fifteen minutes after the appearance of the first three survivors, a second group of men staggered from the smoke-shrouded entrance. Malcolm Link and Charles Jones had been working together in Level 1 North a short distance beyond Wild, Crowther, and Stella. Jones was knocked flat by the force of the explosion, but managed to crawl along the tracks. "I was lucky to get out," he said later. "We men on the North Level were not very far from the entrance and to that, those of us who were rescued owe our lives."

Jack Maddison and John Moorehouse, who were nearly 1,500 feet from the entrance, were knocked from the bench on which they were kneeling. "I heard a loud report," said Maddison, "and realized that something had happened. I made a rush for the chute and up the slope. It was a long walk and I felt very keenly the effect of the gas. At times I felt inclined to lie down but I did not yield to the inclination."

On his way to the surface, he was joined by John Toth, who stumbled from a side tunnel. Together they picked their way through fallen rock and timber, wrecked mine cars, and dead horses.

All along Slant No. 2, dazed men groped their way toward the surface, guided only by their intimate knowledge of the mine and the feeble light from their lamps. From time to time, they stumbled over the dead bodies of fellow miners.

Bill Guthrow, like most of the men in Level 1 North, realized that there had been an explosion, but had no conception of its magnitude. His first instinct was to reach the surface before he met the blackdamp. In his frantic race to freedom, Guthrow caught his boot in a mine track switch and was unable to free himself. His life was probably saved by Moorehouse, who was coming up the slope and stopped to help. With Moorehouse's assistance, Guthrow whipped out his pocketknife and cut the heavy boot from his foot. Then he rejoined the men who were struggling toward safety before the gas overcame them.

Peter Dujay was working close to the bottom of Slant No. 2, some 2,400 feet from the entrance. Though he heard nothing, he was suddenly aware of a concussion and started up the long slope. A short distance along the incline he was joined by engineer Hutchinson and his brother, who were coming out of Level 3 South.

The Hutchinson brothers had been opening that section of the mine for ventilation and were the only two men on that level. Like Dujay, neither had heard the explosion but had felt a sudden rush of air accompanied by falling rock. Knowing that something had happened, they followed the first law of mining and made for the surface.

As the three men started up Slant No. 2 they encountered brown coal smoke so dense that it rendered their lamps almost useless. They knew then that there had been an explosion or fire and that they would certainly encounter blackdamp and afterdamp ahead. Without oxygen masks, their chances of survival were slender. As they made their way up the slope they could sense other men moving near them, but they did not stop.

Evidence of destruction increased as they approached the entrance to Level 1 South. At the entrance they came across the bodies of Rod Wallis and William Neath, the Nova Scotians who on Monday would have been returning to their farm. They now lay dead beneath massive mine timbers. Finally, the brothers stumbled from the mine mouth, gasping for air and collapsing on their knees. At once, the frantic crowd of waiting women and children pressed forward to the rescued miners, presenting a danger almost as great as that of the mine itself.

A pathetically small group of 18 men finally emerged into the glaring sunlight. Of the 235 miners who had gone down, 217 were still trapped in the explosion-wracked, gas-choked tunnels. As the shocked survivors looked at each other, they began to realize that only a miracle could save any of the men still trapped in the shattered tunnels.

One of the rescued, David Murray, scrutinized the coal-blackened faces of the men around him. He saw that none of his three sons, Robert, William, or David Jr., was among them. "Where are my three boys?" he asked.

"They're still down the mine."

Before anyone could stop him, he had wheeled and raced back to the mine entrance.

Constable Hancock, realizing Murray's intentions, grabbed him as he was about to enter the gas-filled corridors. The two men struggled briefly. Murray managed to throw the constable aside and disappeared into the darkness. Neither he nor his sons ever again saw daylight.

Hurry, hurry, hurry

With almost superhuman strength, spurred by the knowledge that even seconds could mean the difference between life and death for those below, men clawed barehanded at the eight-inch blocks of concrete that choked the hoist engine. Under the cool direction of mine manager John Brown, whose two brothers were unaccounted for, they cleared the hoist and the tracks and righted a workable mine car. Almost at the same moment that the frantic father, David Murray, broke loose from Constable Hancock and fled into the chaos, the first rescue car was ready. Among those who rode the first car into danger was engineer Hutchinson, who only moments before had himself emerged, almost overcome by gas and exhaustion.

The first crew, working without oxygen masks, was able to penetrate to the junction of Level 1 North and Level 1 South. Beneath the fallen timbers blocking the entrance to Level 1 South, they found the bodies of Rod Wallis and William Neath. Pushing into Level 1 North, they heard the laboured breathing of three men and passed them back to the mine car, which whisked them to the surface, together with the bodies of Wallis and Neath. It was now 10:00 a.m. and the government rescue car had arrived from Blairmore in the charge of D.S. Hyslop, who brought the welcome news that nearly 100 miners were also on their way. Among supplies on the rescue car were oxygen masks, which were rushed to the mine entrance. At the same time, an emergency tent hospital was set up in the mine yard under Dr. William Dodd of the Hillcrest Hospital.

The rescue team wore masks to protect them from blackdamp.

With the masks, Hutchinson and his party were able to push deeper into Level 1 North. Within minutes they brought another group of men overcome by blackdamp to the surface. They found the entrance to Level 1 South blocked with fallen debris, but managed to force their way through twisted track and smashed mine cars. Inside they found 30 men face down in water. All were dead.

Further down Slant No. 2, another group of rescuers cleared debris from the second level. Almost at once their heroic efforts were rewarded. They came upon a group of survivors.

"I was working some distance inside No. 2 South," said Joseph Atkinson, one of the first rescued. "I didn't hear the report of the explosion. It was just as if I had suddenly gone deaf, or as if two four-inch nails had been driven into my ears. That's how it felt. I was bowled over by the shock but scrambled to my feet."

The shock of the blast was followed by a wave of brown smoke coming from Slant No. 1. It drove Atkinson and his fellow workers back. Sensing that the explosion had taken place in that vicinity, they turned and raced toward Slant No. 2. They found one miner on hands and knees groping along the corridor and tried to carry him, but already, deadly gases had invaded that section of the mine. They had to drop him and stagger on. Before they could reach the entrance to Slant No. 2, they encountered a solid wall of deadly blackdamp that drove them back.

"We lay down and rolled back with what strength we had left to a pool of water about 50 or 60 feet back, and there we crawled into the water, soaking our shirts and sucking them to keep off the effects of the afterdamp."

Gustaf Franz, unable to keep his head from falling into the water, was drowned. One by one the men fell unconscious. Atkinson's last recollection was of seeing a short distance away the body of a miner cut almost in two by the blast.

It was this group of men that engineer Hutchinson found and brought to the surface. They were rushed to the hospital tent and given oxygen. All revived.

Hutchinson, meanwhile, returned to the mine. Although the intricate network of tunnels and passageways caused confusion as to where the explosions had occurred, it became apparent that the initial explosion had taken place near Level 1 South and Slant No. 1. Here the greatest destruction had occurred. Between Slant No. 1 and Slant No. 2, however, the smoke and rushing air wound through the tunnels in such weird and confusing patterns that men trying to read the danger signals ran toward death rather than away from it. One group of nearly 50 men who escaped death from the initial blasts groped their way toward the entrance to Mine No. 1, only to find their exit blocked. There they were overtaken by blackdamp as they turned and tried to make their way back to Slant No. 2. All died.

Some were more fortunate. "I was working some distance in from the mouth of Slant No. 2 when the explosion occurred," said Herbert Yeadon. "It sounded somewhat like the discharge of a big gun on a battleship."

On coming out of the tunnel where he was working, Yeadon saw two men lying dead in a passageway leading to Slant No. 2. When moments later he saw men running toward him from that direction, he assumed that the explosion had taken place near Slant No. 2 and that the men were running from it. He, and several nearby miners, turned and ran toward Slant No. 1.

A short distance from Yeadon's tunnel, the fleeing miners encountered blackdamp and turned back, frantically searching for pools of water into which they could dip their clothing. By breathing through their wet clothes and sucking in the water they could obtain sufficient oxygen to sustain life. Believing that the centre of the explosion was in Slant No. 2, their only hope lay in being found by rescue workers.

One by one the men around Yeadon lapsed into unconsciousness. Some never awakened, while others were restored to life on hospital cots as anxious friends and relatives watched over them. Meanwhile, in Level 1 North, which had almost completely escaped the force of the explosions and where the intake fans had provided air, rescue work proceeded rapidly. Within an hour the last of the miners in that section had been brought to the surface alive.

By 11:30 a.m., 40 men had either escaped under their own power or been brought out unconscious. With every passing moment, however, the pall of horror deepened around the mine entrance. Men, women, and children slowly accepted the fact that only a series of miracles could help the remaining 198 men assumed to be in the death pit.

Two miracles did occur.

The first was the discovery by Robert Hood of the two brass checks he had absent-mindedly hung on their hooks early that morning. The two men he had sent home were safe. Their safety reduced the probable casualty list to 196, a figure that was announced publicly and appeared in early editions of many newspapers.

Shortly after 11:30 a.m., a squad of rescuers, under the direction of the indefatigable Hutchinson, fought its way through the debris of Level 1 South and discovered Herbert Yeadon and his companions. Only Yeadon and six others showed signs of life. They were rushed to the surface, where all seven survived.

By noon, miracles had ceased. Of the 235 men who had gone down the mine that morning, only 46 remained alive, some of them barely breathing. Of the 189 others, the bodies of only 26 had been brought to the surface. Among them was David Murray, the father who had escaped but plunged back into the devastation in an effort to find his three sons.

Although a number of men had been rescued, engineer Hutchinson was the only one with sufficient knowledge of the mine workings to give any clear picture of what had happened. Fireboss John Ironmonger was still unconscious; fireboss Sam Charlton was unaccounted for; mine superintendent James S. Quigley, pit boss Thomas Taylor, and other men who had intimate knowledge of the mine were still missing. From the information sent back by Hutchinson, a picture of conditions around Slant No. 2 was formed, but nothing was known about Slant No. 1.

A work crew was organized to unblock the choked throat of the rock tunnel, and finally a hole was cleared large enough for one man to crawl through. Selected was Harry White, a former fireboss who had arrived with the rescuers from the other mines. Wearing an oxygen helmet and carrying spare oxygen on his back, he wormed his way through the narrow opening and dropped to the floor of Slant No. 1.

Men, horses, timber, and mine cars were strewn in a chaotic mass. Mine tracks had been torn loose and bent into grotesque shapes. Between the mouth of the mine and Level 1 South, White counted the bodies of 26 men, some horribly disfigured by the explosion. Some, like Thomas Bardsley, had been transfixed in death—crouching, kneeling, walking. All had their lamps blown away.

As he approached tunnel 32, the evidence of destruction became greatest. From tunnels 31 to 35, the miners had been badly burned and disfigured.

There he found fireboss Sam Charlton, the firing cable still wrapped around his body. The battery was lying a few feet away, but the key necessary to activate the battery was missing. Later it was found in Charlton's pocket, and the two unexploded charges discovered in tunnel 32.

In the next tunnel, 33, the signs of destruction were the most obvious. White concluded that something had taken place in 33 that had made Sam Charlton hesitate and withhold detonating the charges in 32.

Later, engineer Hutchinson arrived at the same conclusion after his examination of 33. Fireboss Daniel Briscoe, however, was equally positive that the explosion had originated a little farther along the level, somewhere between tunnels 35 and 45. Whatever the point of origin, the devastation was so severe that no indication of the cause was clear. The only definite conclusion was that it could not have been caused by Sam Charlton.

Pushing his way through the cave-ins and rockfalls, White came across 30 bodies—victims of blackdamp. They were in a side tunnel scarcely 50 feet from the blocked entrance to the mine.

Shocked families camped on the coal-soaked hillside waited in hopes that a husband, son, or brother would emerge alive.

It was a disheartening report that he made to manager John Brown. He had seen no signs of life in any of the sections of the mines north of Slant No. 1. The only encouraging aspect was his discovery that severe though the explosion had been, there were no fires burning.

Identifying the dead

Even under ideal conditions, the Hillcrest Mine property was not pretty. The mountainside looked as if some mad barber had shaved clean the area around the mine entrance, leaving a stubble of blackened tree trunks. The once-brown soil was stained charcoal by the constant rain of coal dust, and the once-white rocks jutting from the stripped slopes were ugly black smudges. When RNWMP Inspector Christen Junget arrived from Pincher Creek at 11:30 a.m. to take charge of police operations, the scene resembled Dante's Inferno.

Dazed women, frightened children tagging at their heels, wandered aimlessly or sat dejectedly on coal-soiled mine equipment, unconscious

Rescuers brought the dead out of the wrecked mine.

of the damage to their clothing. When anyone came out of the mine, they rushed forward for a glimpse of what the mine car carried—perhaps a breath of information, of hope. Sadly, there was only despair.

After a brief consultation with mine officials, Inspector Junget relieved corporals Grant and Mead and detailed them to the wash house, replacing them with Corporal Searle and Constable Stanley Kistruck. Constable Hancock was assigned to collecting evidence for identification.

Six gangs of rescuers were at work in the mine, but their progress was slow. Only the men killed instantly were at their stations. The others had swarmed through the passages, vainly trying to find a way out

Men unloaded bodies into the wash house, where they were matched with missing parts, washed, searched for identification, and wrapped in shrouds. Although drinking was suspended in the town, a miraculous bottle of whiskey placed in the wash house for the volunteers carrying out the grisly task never seemed to go dry.

of the deadly labyrinth. Each nook and cranny had to be searched, and many of the tunnels were sealed off with fallen rock or timbers.

The bodies of 26 men already brought up were carried to the wash house and placed in the charge of Mead and Grant. With a group of miners assisting, they washed the bodies and searched clothing for identification tags. In many instances the men were so disfigured that identification was impossible.

As the afternoon deepened, order was restored out of the tragic chaos. The grief-stricken crowds left the mine yard and gathered around the wash house and the Miners' Hall. Only then did the most difficult part of the rescue work begin. Despite the anxious women and children waiting at the mine entrance, the rescuers had deliberately left many of the most badly mangled bodies inside, fearful lest the dismembered corpses unnerve the survivors. As the crowd thinned, the men began to bring up parts of bodies and hastily sent the pieces into the concrete wash house, where the police tried to match bodies and limbs.

As the rescuers probed deeper into the mine, braving the continual danger of another explosion, they came upon small groups of bodies huddled around small pockets of water, all victims of blackdamp. When they were brought to the surface, the gas had to be pressed from them—usually in the wash house—and after a few hours the smell of gas hovered constantly inside the walls. Fortunately, Inspector Junget was a man of discernment, and a bottle of whiskey appeared on one of the shelves. It was a rather miraculous bottle that never seemed to run completely dry.

By dusk, all realized that none of the remaining men below were alive.

One more person was almost added to this sad statistic. Robert Levitt, a miner who had arrived with the rescue crew from Bellevue, had gone into the mine without an oxygen mask, relying on the fans that had restored much of the air. Alone, he had ventured up a passageway to search for victims. When he tried to find his way back through the unfamiliar tunnels, he became lost and encountered a pocket of blackdamp. When the other members of the search party noted his absence and started a search, they found him unconscious. On the surface he lay near death for half an hour before the pulmotor revived him.

When darkness fell, all remaining hope for those below was officially given up. Under cover of night, Constable Hancock moved into the mine to search for missing legs and arms.

At 11:30 p.m., one of the rescue parties came across a fire burning in the mine. All crews were immediately recalled and placed on standby while a firefighting party went below. When the fire was quelled, the miners moved through the tunnels methodically searching for victims. One of the men encountered a pile of mine timbers and saw by the light of his lamp six or seven men dead in an alcove. Unable to reach them he could only mark the place for a later attempt.

In the wash house, corporals Mead and Grant worked steadily, their senses numbed by the horror of their task. As bodies were cleaned and assembled, they were wrapped in white shrouds and placed in wagons. Under the escort of other constables they were taken to the Miners' Hall and laid out in rows. When the Miners' Hall was filled, the upper story of George Cruickshank's General Store was requisitioned.

There had never been any feeling of goodwill between the miners and the police, but as the miners watched the three police officers work hour after hour without food, rest, or relief, an official of the United Mine Workers Union said: "We have no use for the police, but we cannot help respecting its members when we see them working under such trying conditions."

Alert to the possibility of trouble if general drinking was allowed, Inspector Junget had the local hotel's licence suspended. The whiskey bottle on the shelf in the wash house, however, continued to reproduce discreetly and promptly.

At 3:00 a.m. the rescue teams were again removed from the tunnels when a search team discovered another fire deeper in the mine. When it seemed that the mine was doomed, a call came for more firefighters. In spite of the possible danger of another explosion from flames skipping along the ribbons of methane gas and encountering coal dust, more men went into the mine. They were too tired to be heroes. They just wanted to finish their gloomy task.

The fire was brought under control just before dawn. Then the rescue teams, most of them without sleep for 24 hours, resumed their search of the underground maze for more victims.

By Saturday noon, 162 bodies had been viewed by a coroner's jury of 10 miners and passed for burial. Still other segmented bodies were awaiting completion in the wash house. The underground searchers

Coffins lay lined up on the ground as mourners consoled each other and said their last goodbyes.

had reached the destruction-ridden section around tunnels 32 and 33 in Old Level 1. Here their progress was slow. There were fewer bodies and more fragments.

Three huge graves

Sunday, June 21, 1914, dawned cold and blustery. Dense white mists rolled over the valley floor between Hillcrest and Bellevue, while a chilling wind whipped snowflakes into the faces of men completing the last of three huge graves. Even as the first light filtered through the windows, people were stirring. Some slipped away to the Miners' Hall or Cruickshank's Store for a last look before the coffins were nailed shut. Others harnessed horses to carts, wagons, and democrats for use as hearses. Still others merely sat and stared blankly into the uncertain future.

Under the supervision of the undertaker, the coffins were laid out in rows on a vacant lot next to the General Store. Among those who passed by was Fernand Capron, a 12-year-old boy who had arrived from Belgium only the day before. As his father guided him between rows of coffins with their grieving attendants, he said: "Son, take note of this and never go down the mines."

At 10:00 a.m., funeral services began, Father Beaton officiating for Roman Catholics and Reverend Watkins for Anglicans. When they were completed, the hearses moved forward. With the Bellevue Band playing "Saul's Dead March," the little procession started down the winding road and disappeared into the mist-shrouded valley. Then at 1:00 p.m., union services began under the auspices of Reverend Young, assisted by eight other ministers. As the coffins were loaded onto the waiting wagons, the crowds around Cruickshank's Store diminished. Finally the vacant lot was empty of people and coffins.

As if the sombre funeral processions were not enough, a macabre touch was added when a team of horses bolted, dumping their load of coffins by the roadside. Some of the wood caskets burst open, spilling

With the Bellevue Band playing "Saul's Dead March," the funeral procession started down the winding road toward the mist-shrouded valley.

the bodies on the ground. The mourners, already numbed by the ter-
ror of the past three days, quickly restored order and moved on toward
the waiting mass graves.

By nightfall, 150 men had been laid to rest in the cemetery at
the foot of Turtle Mountain. In the following days, the remains of
William Fines, Fred Bennett, and Herbert Adlam were placed in the
hillside cemetery at Blairmore. Rod Wallis, William Neath, and the
bodies of four other miners were escorted to Nova Scotia by Andrew
Wallis and his sister. Transportation was given without charge by the
Canadian Pacific Railway as far as Saint John, New Brunswick, then the
Intercolonial Railway carried them to their respective towns.

Scarcely a day passed in the following two weeks that was not
marked by a small funeral cortege along the winding road to the cemetery. The bulk of miners who lost their lives were married—an estimated 130 left widows, and most had children. Mine superintendents
James Quigley and David Walker each left a wife and six children.

The dead were interred in three mass graves, the largest being 200 feet long.

Charles Elick left a youthful family, the youngest born the day after the tragedy. In all, some 400 children, most under 10, were made fatherless by the tragedy.

The families of those killed were entitled to $1,800 compensation from Hillcrest Collieries. Processing claims took time, however, and the need for immediate help was pressing. A local relief committee was formed, with a relief centre opened in Hillcrest. Relief offices were established in most cities of the Canadian west and various city councils voted grants to the stricken families. In addition, from the federal government came a grant of $50,000 and from the province of Alberta another $20,000.

In the meantime, corporals Mead and Grant, with Constable Hancock, had completed their grim task of identifying bodies. For a week they lived, ate, and slept in the wash house with its continuous parade of mangled bodies. Once the majority of bodies had been recovered, they spent hours searching the workings with miners, trying to locate parts of bodies and pieces of personal property. In many areas of the mine the debris still prevented proper search, but within a week after the maelstrom of death, all but two bodies had been recovered.

Right: *Joseph Atkinson, shown here with his wife many years later, was one of those rescued in the Hillcrest mine disaster.*

Below: *Charles Ironmonger Jr. was not so lucky. He was one of the youngest miners to die at Hillcrest.*

In recognition, all three men were awarded a special sum of $50 for their courageous work. Constable Hancock, who earned 60 cents a day, was awed by this bonus of almost three months' pay. Promotions for all followed shortly.

On July 7, 1914, a rescue team found one of the still-missing miners. He was Joseph Oakley, identified by the brass tag in his pocket. There remained only one brass check still unaccounted for in the timekeeper's office—that of Sidney Bainbridge. Years later, a retired Constable Hancock supplied the story of the missing miner.

Many of the bodies brought from the mine were without arms, legs or heads. The three policemen had striven valiantly to match limbs to torsos but, finally, one leg remained. The obvious conclusion was that Sidney Bainbridge had caught the full force of the blast and all that remained of his body was one leg. Without drawing undue attention, the police officers slipped the extra leg into one of the coffins and sealed it. Thus, one coffin bore the remains of two miners.

An official inquiry into the disaster revealed considerable disagreement about the cause of the explosion. All the firebosses affirmed that the Hillcrest workings were relatively safe—having neither an unusual amount of gas nor coal dust. By contrast, District Inspector of Mines Francis Aspinall testified that in his opinion, the mine was both gaseous and dusty. Some witnesses stated that the explosion could have been caused by a pick throwing sparks from a rock; others felt that such sparks would be insufficient to start a fire. Lost in all the words was the quiet testimony of Harry White, the first man to traverse the mine from end to end while the ravages of the blast were still fresh.

In White's opinion, the explosion had occurred in tunnel 33 when sparks from a rockfall ignited the ever-present methane gas. This fire resulted in the subsequent deadly explosion of coal dust. His theory was ignored. Twelve years later, however, he was to be vindicated.

Samples of coal dust from the mines had been submitted to the U.S. Bureau of Mines in Washington for testing. In his final report on October 24, 1914, Commissioner A.A. Carpenter stated that the dust from the mines was of a highly explosive nature. As a result, Carpenter reported that a gas explosion of unknown origin had triggered a coal-dust explosion, or several explosions.

Earlier, on July 23, a coroner's jury at Coleman had rendered a verdict in which they stated that they did not think the company had adhered strictly to the regulations of the Coal Mines Act. The jury also criticized the government Mine Inspection Branch for not inspecting mines more frequently, and the Safety Committee of the Hillcrest Mine Union for not having adequate safety apparatus on hand in case of accident.

Whatever the various verdicts and opinions, one tragic fact remained—189 men died in the most terrible explosion in the history of Canadian mining.

The years after

The evening of September 19, 1926, was light and warm as fireboss Frank Lote left the mine office and descended into Hillcrest mine through the rock tunnel. Below, in the clustered houses of the village, 150 men were making final preparations to climb the hill and start the night shift. Following the 1914 disaster, improved mining methods and more modern safety apparatus reduced fears of another coal-dust explosions. With every fatality-free year, the feeling of safety and security grew. But only a miracle on this day prevented upwards of 150 more miners dying from a massive explosion or the deadly blackdamp.

Frank Lote completed his rounds in the lower depths and started along Level 6 South, which would bring him to Slant No. 2. Here the only other man in the mine, Fred Jones, was tending the pumping system between Levels 2 and 3 South.

It was 10:20 p.m.

Somewhere in the depths of the mine, rocks fell from a tunnel roof, struck sparks and ignited the methane gas. The flame skipped along the timbers and struck coal dust.

A thunderous explosion came from behind Frank Lote, killing him instantly. Even as billows of brown smoke cascaded over his inert form, the deadly fingers poked through the labyrinth of passageways, seeking other victims. A surge of air rushed up Slant No. 2, bowling Fred Jones over and knocking his safety lamp from his head.

Within minutes, a rescue party was formed at the mine entrance by mine inspector M. Johnson. Equipped with the latest safety devices, the men plunged into the smoke shrouded wreckage. On every side they saw that the explosion had caused greater devastation than the 1914 explosion. Timbers were blasted to pieces, mine cars crunched, and iron rails kinked like fine wires. This time, fortunately, they were looking for two men, not 235.

They found Fred Jones some 900 feet down the slope of Slant No. 2, his body limp, overcome by blackdamp. But it was three days before they discovered the clue to Frank Lote's whereabouts. While gangs of miners worked around the clock to repair the damage to the mine's interior, the rescue party found Lote's lamp lying in a pool of water in No. 6 Level South.

This time the evidence was clear. No spark from a miner's pick, no sudden flaring of a lamp, no unwise blasting had caused this upheaval. The only cause remaining was a rockfall. Those who had listened to Harry White's quiet testimony at the inquiry into Canada's worst disaster in 1914 wondered if the miner had been right after all. If so, no amount of safety precautions would ever render Hillcrest Collieries safe. Nothing could guarantee that in the miles and miles of mine workings rocks would not fall, or that the mine would be empty when they did.

Nevertheless, within a month the mine was again functioning.

Bratticemen roved the dark passageways directing the flow of air through the workings, miners dug, and firebosses blasted, and carpenters hammered away in the bowels of Hillcrest Mountain. The days grew into months, the months into years. Finally, on December 1, 1949, the historic old mine closed because it was no longer competitive.

Charges of dynamite sealed forever the rock tunnel and the dirt entrance to Mine No. 2. The formidable tipple that overlooked the village of Hillcrest was torn down and transported to other mines in the area. Mine cars, tracks, and machinery were removed to serve other mines or other purposes. With the passage of the years the roofs of the engine room and the wash house caved in.

Today, nothing remains but graceful ruins.

More than 150 victims of the Hillcrest mine disaster lay buried in this mass grave.

*A lichen-covered headstone marks
the grave of one of the fallen miners.*

In Memoriam

Ackers, Peter
Adlam, Herbert
Albenese, Dominic
Albenese, Nicholas
Anderson, Robert
Andreaschuk, Jacob
Androski, George
Armstrong, James
Bainbridge, Sidney
Banlant, Andrew
Banyar, Steve
Barber, James
Bardsley, Thomas
Bennett, Fred C.
Bingham, Fred
Bodio, Virgilio
Bolinski, John
Botter, Etalleredo
Bostock, Frank M.
Bowie, John S.
Bozzer, Pietro
Bradshaw, James
Brown, John

Brown, Thomas W.
Brown, William
Buckman, Albert
Camarda, Joseph
Cantalline, Peter
Carelli, Antonio
Carr, Henry
Cassagrande, Carlo
Cataline, Sam
Catanio, Antonio
Caterino, Basso
Celli, Vito
Chabillon, Emil
Chabillon, Leonce
Charles, Charles S.
Charlton, Sam
Ciccone, Eugenio
Cimetta, Antonio
Clarke, John
Clarke, Leonard
Coan, Charles
Corkill, Thomas
Coulter, Fred

Coulter, Robert
Court, Thompson
Cullinen, Dan
Daye, Prosper
Davidson, John
Demchuk, George
Demchuk, Nicholas
Dickenson, Matthew
Dugdale, Andrew
Dugdale, Robert
Elick, Charles
Emery, David
Eveloir, Everard
Ewing, James
Fedoruk, Peter
Fines, William
Flourgere, August
Fogale, John C.
Fortunato, Luigi
Fortunato, Vincenzo
Foster, John
Fox, William
Francz, Gustaf

Frech, Frank
Gallimore, William
Garine, Emil
Gasperion, Antonio
Gianoli, Carlo
Gramacci, Antonio
Gray, James F.
Guido, Ylio
Hansford, Ralph
Harris, David G.
Heber, John
Heusdens, Alphonse
Hicken, George
Hillman, William
Hnacnuk, Philip
Hood, John
Hunter, Hugh
Iluk, Wasyl
Ironmonger, Charles
Ironmonger, Sam
Janego, Mike
Johnson, Carl
Johnson, Fred
Johnson, William
Kane, Pat
Kinock, Peter
Kipryanchuk, Mike
Kohar, Petro
Kosmik, Chris
Kostynuk, Dan
Kurigatz, Fred
Kuzenko, Nick
Kwasnico, Fred
Kwasnico, Wasyl
Labonne, Frank
Legard, Antoine
Melanchuk, Steve
Marchetto, Ulderico
Marcolli, Guiseppi
Megency, Nicholas
Meiklejohn, Adam

Melok, John
Miller, William
Miller, William G.
Montelli, Dominic
Morley, William
Moore, William
Morrison, Alex
Morron, Nick
Mudrik, John
Muir, Robert
Muirhouse, Fred
Murray, David Sr.
Murray, David Jr.
Murray, William
Murray, Robert
Myrovich, Steve
Mclssac, Rod
McKay, Angus H.
McKinnon, John B.
McKinnon, Steve
NcNeil, Pius
McQuarrie, John A.
Neath, William
Oakley, Joseph
Pagnan, Eduardo
Pardegtt, Arthur
Parnisari, Carlo
Parnisari, Guiseppi
Payet, Leon
Pearson, John
Penn, James
Penn, Robert
Petrie, Alex
Petrie, James
Petrie, Robert
Porteous, Alex
Porteous, James
Pounder, George
Quigley, James S.
Quigley, Thomas
Raitko, Steve

Ralnyk, Bernard
Ralnyk, Fred
Rees, Albert
Robertson, George
Rochester, Joseph H.
Rochester, William
Rossanese, Eugenio
Rosti, Luigi
Sands, John
Sandul, John
Sandulik, Daniel
Schroeder, Charles
Silva, Alfred
Skurhan, Mike
Smith, Robert
Smith, Thomas
Somotink, Peter
Southwell, Albert
Stretton, Edward
Tamborini, Albert
Tamborini, Baldo
Taylor, Thomas
Thaczuk, John
Thomas, Deo
Trump, William
Turner, Thomas
Turner, William
Tyron, Mike
Vendrasco, Fred
Vohradsky, Joseph
Vohradsky, Vince
Walker, David J.
Wallis, Rod
Wilson, Thomas L.
Zahara, John
Zamis, Luis
Zapisocki, Wasyl
Zaska, Michael

FERNIE: CITY
UNDER A CURSE

Elsie Turnbull

T he city of Fernie is a prosperous and tranquil-looking community of some 5,000 amid snowy peaks in the B.C. section of the Crowsnest Pass. Its tranquil appearance is misleading, however, since its history records more tragedies than any other community in the pass, a region where disaster has struck frequently and brutally. While other Crowsnest communities such as Bellevue, Hillcrest, Frank, and Coleman have escaped with one major calamity, Fernie has experienced a series. They range from mine explosions, one alone killing 128 men, to fires, the worst being a conflagration that left virtually all 6,000 residents homeless.

While the general reasons for these disasters point to man's carelessness or nature's excesses, there are those who blame the "curse" for the disasters that have befallen the community. According to legend, the curse originated when a group of men were prospecting for minerals near Crowsnest Mountain. Among them was William Fernie, after whom the community is named. One night prior to the 1890s when the prospecting group was camped beside an Indian band, Fernie noticed that the chief's daughter was wearing a necklace of shiny black stones. He recognized them as pieces of coal. Thwarted in his effort to find their source, he wooed the Indian girl and learned her secret. Then he deserted her. In great anger her mother invoked a curse on the

Elk River Valley and all its inhabitants "who will suffer from fire, flood, strife and discord; all will finally die from fire and water!"

Whether the story of the widely believed curse was of Indian or white invention is not known, nor whether Fernie was the unfaithful Romeo. The latter is highly unlikely, however, since in the Crowsnest Pass coal wasn't hidden or hard to find. It was, in fact, so common that prospectors searching for gold complained about "coal, coal, everywhere." So much was evident that the region was christened "nature's coal bin."

If there is doubt about Fernie's involvement with the curse, there is none about another aspect of his life. He was among the first to begin systematically prospecting for coal and one of a group that in 1889 organized the Crow's Nest Coal and Mineral Company. It received a charter to build a railway through the pass and in 1897 made an arrangement with the Canadian Pacific Railway, which in 1898 built the B.C. Southern. The original Crow's Nest Coal and Mineral Company changed its name to Crow's Nest Pass Coal Company and began large-scale mining. Fernie later sold his interest and moved to Victoria. If there was a curse he wasn't affected. He lived to be 84 and left an estate of nearly $300,000, a huge fortune for the times.

The Crow's Nest Pass Coal Company grew quickly. Their 250,000 acres of land west of the Elk River contained over 80 seams of coal, enabling them to produce varying grades—blacksmithing, coking, bituminous, steam, and semi-anthracite. By the end of 1897, the firm had opened No. 1 tunnel on the north side and No. 2 tunnel on the south side of Coal Creek. Situated five miles from the Elk River, the mines were in a narrow valley bounded by steep hills that virtually blocked the winter sun, with avalanches always a threat.

Headquarters of the company was at Fernie, a CPR station on the flats bordering Elk River where 200 beehive-shaped coke ovens were built, as well as a branch rail line to the mines at Coal Creek. Not far from the ovens, two rows of shacks "of unbarked logs" were the first buildings in what would be "Old Fernie."

Within a year the townsite of Fernie was laid out across the CPR tracks. The new community grew quickly and in 1900, a Montreal writer who identified himself only as "W.B. McB." wrote:

"Fernie presents a remarkable example of the way western towns are built up. Three years ago what is now the site of the town was a dense forest of Douglas fir, cedar and spruce. In the following year a 'shack town' sprang up with the advent of the railway and commencement of mining activity. At that time it was wild and lawless, but presented splendid opportunities for making money.

"Now though only about two years old, it is a town of over 2,000 inhabitants with a park, athletic grounds, skating rink, four or five churches and several very good hotels. It is quite well supplied with modern conveniences, such as electric lights and waterworks, and there is a wide awake enterprising spirit about the place that seems strange to a steady-going easterner."

In December 1901 the *Fernie Free Press* reported with satisfaction:

"The population of Fernie today is 3,000, which entitles it to be regarded as the third largest town in the interior of the Province of British Columbia, Rossland coming first and Nelson second. At the present rate of progress, Fernie will in the course of two years pass both; there is little doubt that this will be the case since there is no element of speculation in the mineral development of the town.

"With the program sketched out by the large corporation doing business here, it is not too much to expect that a few years will see Fernie with a population of 10,000, and a coal and coke industry of such

A visitor wrote that Fernie (seen here in 1902) seemed to have a "wide-awake enterprising spirit."

dimensions as will place it ahead of any mineral camp in the Province."

Less than six months later the paper recorded the first in what would be a series of mine disasters. Like other mines in the Crowsnest Pass, Coal Creek was dangerous because of the gas and fine coal dust. The Montreal writer had been taken on a tour of the mine and wrote:

"When the gas is present in large enough proportions it gradually fills the room, and when ignited forms a solid mass of flame, and I have frequently seen men terribly burned by it though the fire lasted only a few seconds. Sometimes, too, it forms in such large quantities that when mixed with air it gives rise to violent explosions in which many lives are lost. At Salt Lake City, Utah, last summer 200 lives were lost. So far no lives have been lost in Fernie, in this way, which is rather remarkable, as open lights are used almost exclusively."

The mine's good fortune ended on May 22, 1902, when an explosion ripped through No. 2 mine with such force that "while funeral trains were assembled to take the bodies down to Fernie … some were so mangled that they were taken right to the burial ground." Of the disaster, the *Fernie Free Press* reported:

"About 7 o'clock on the evening of May 22, 1902, a cloud of smoke, gas, and dust shot 1,000 feet into the air from the fanhouse on No. 2 mine, followed by a shrill unscheduled whistle from the Coal Creek plant. These marked an explosion in the depths of No. 2 and adjoining No. 3 mines which snuffed out the lives of 128 men, almost the whole working shift. Not a man out of the 90 employed in the shaft of No. 2 mine lived to tell the tale but in No. 3, 20 survivors had escaped from the left side of the slope …

"Within 12 minutes rescuers were at hand but found that the pipes in the roof of the tunnel which conducted air throughout the mine had been destroyed. It was impossible to enter the mine until these were repaired. For six hours they worked, every few moments a man collapsing and another taking his place. About 2 a.m. they found the first body, Joe Sengala, and a moment later Stephen Morgan. Neither had any marks. At 4 a.m. work had to be suspended for several hours to let the gas escape. All day Friday the search continued. By 6 o'clock, 31 had been taken out but a fall of rock delayed getting the last bodies for several days. Townspeople fell in behind the wagons carrying bodies to their graves while a newspaperman wrote: 'Fernie is in a condition of gloom and resounds with the hopeless cries of widows and orphans.'"

Townspeople fell in behind the wagons carrying 28 bodies to their graves. A newspaperman wrote: "Fernie is in a condition of gloom and resounds with the hopeless cries of widows and orphans."

Shortly after the 1902 explosion, the first miners' strike occurred at Coal Creek Colliery, when a new manager roused hostility by extending the day's work from eight to eight and a half hours. The strike lasted seven weeks but unfortunately for the miners, resulted in almost unconditional surrender.

The year 1902 also resulted in a near disaster when summer brought a serious outbreak of typhoid from polluted water. Fortunately, the disease was arrested when Fernie's water intake was changed from below the mine discharge to above.

Two years later a fire devastated the community, wiping out almost the entire commercial centre. It broke out in the early morning of April 30 in C. Richard's general store, and by 8 a.m. the whole block was smouldering embers. But the community quickly recovered, and the "embers had hardly cooled before the sound of carpenters' hammers were heard."

Fernie was incorporated as a city in July 1904, the first city council passing many measures that they hoped would help prevent destructive fires. Among new buildings was one built by the Crow's Nest Pass

Coal Company, a massive stone office set well back from the street. Four years later when Fernie was engulfed by a massive conflagration, the stone office was to be an oasis amid block after block of ashes.

Before then, however, there had been a range of other disasters. The first was another major fire in 1905. It started in George Carruther's tailor shop, located in a room of the *Free Press* building, and destroyed a town block worth $80,000. J.R. Wallace, later owner and editor of the newspaper, slept above Carruther's shop and had a narrow escape. Waking from sleep, he noticed flames coming up around the stovepipe. He grabbed his clothes and fled, picking up some galleys of type and a few other small items. That was all that was saved of the printing plant. A month later another block of wooden buildings burned, with damage this time some $40,000.

That same year two mine tipple buildings caught fire. Next morning nothing remained but hot ashes and twisted iron. While the destroyed tipple buildings were replaced by a single steel structure, the fire resulted in No. 3 mine being flooded. It remained closed for nearly four years.

In 1906 residents were free of serious fires, but for those with relatives in the mines there was an ominous development. There occurred the first of many "bumps," which would become a deadly factor in subsequent disasters in Coal Creek mines. Technically, a bump is the coming together of roof and floor within a mine, probably due to geologic stress. At the time officials at Coal Creek could not pinpoint the cause.

For the next two years these bumps continued with no serious results. Then on July 31, 1908, a big bump in No. 2 mine at Coal Creek killed three miners and imprisoned 20 others for eight hours. Of the 20, one who was taken out alive with no bodily injuries died later from shock. As a result of the deadly bump, all the shafts of the active area of No. 2 mine were abandoned.

Before shocked townspeople could bury the victims of the bump, a greater disaster unfurled. For 10 days that July, the town had been clouded with smoke from a bush fire burning in logging debris at the Cedar Valley Lumber Company's mill near West Fernie. It was not considered dangerous until a brisk wind sprang up about two o'clock on Saturday morning, August 1. The slash fire suddenly became a monster that wiped out the Cedar Valley mill, then a volcano of flame, which advanced on Fernie. At the Dairy Ranch the flames split, one all-consuming tongue roaring eastward along the Great Northern

Railway, the other to the west, its mass easily leaping the barrier of the Elk River. In West Fernie the fire department valiantly fought to check the blaze at the Elk Lumber Company, which had 6 million board feet of lumber in the yards.

The department's effort was futile. Mill and lumber became a massive inferno, the gale-force wind carrying embers and even burning lumber into the city.

The Fernie, Central, and Waldorf Hotels were quickly blazing, as was the Opera House, its roof blown off and carried a block by the super-hot wind before the fire even reached it. Townspeople fled, many barely able to keep ahead of the flames. Later the *Free Press* noted that many survivors had been "… scorched and blistered by whirling flames, blinded by smoke, crazed by separation from loved ones and fleeing they knew not where, checked by walls of flame just as safety seemed at hand, confused by the suddenness of the catastrophe and

Faster than a galloping horse, the volcano of flame and smoke advanced on Fernie, destroying this Catholic Church and 1,000 other buildings.

faint with seemingly futile exertion!" People of Old Town, most of them foreigners, had to be driven toward the north by cool-headed men, the crying, screaming mothers praying and carrying children. Two hundred people crowded into the stone office of the Crow's Nest Pass Coal Company, another 60 women and children took refuge in the Western Canada Wholesale Warehouse, while men on the roof kept the shingles wet.

Without the coal company's office as a refuge, many of the 200 who found safety there would probably have died. As Mayor W.W. Tuttle remarked later: "A man on a horse couldn't have kept ahead of the fire."

One graphic account was written by a miner named William Richard Puckey, who had a few hours previously helped remove one of the three miners killed by the bump at No. 2 mine. He left Coal Creek on the train and remembered:

"When we were within one mile of Fernie we came upon French Camp that was two rows of wooden houses, built along each side of the track. They were all ablaze together, and into that blazing hell the engineer dashed, with one coach and the flatcar with the reels on.

"I shouted, 'Put handkerchiefs over nose and mouth.' When we got through, the coach was all afire and the city was all on fire together.

"Men, women and children were fleeing in all directions, calling for help. The sight of it will never be forgotten by those who went through it all. One family in particular, a Mr. David Murray, wife and 10 children were leaving for the Old Home, Scotland. When we got to Fernie both Mr. and Mrs. Murray had lost their nerves. She threw five children through an open window and Mr. Murray pulled her through. Mr. Murray grabbed two boys and I got two more. Mrs. Murray got the little girl, then we called on the others to follow, and I rushed off, heading for the river.

"I hailed a passing team, and got them all piled on, and told the driver to drive to either station, the CPR or the GN. I then went to look for the others, but it was in vain. Fires were springing up all around us, the smoke was choking, and there were other women and children to save ...

"Great big trees were torn up as if by unseen hands, and the sun, when it pierced the clouds, shone down like a ball of fire. Fires sprang up wherever it shone for a second, but there happened to be two engines at the depot, and the crews soon had a line of empty boxcars ready.

"Into these we packed all the women and children until we had about 30 (boxcars) loaded. Then the fires were beginning to warm us up all around, and you could not see for smoke. Then we pulled out of the burning city, but on all sides of us fires were burning. After going about five miles, we got to a place where, to get the line level, they had cut away from the base of one of the mountains here.

"The train pulled up, and 1,500 people rushed from the boxcars to the river's edge. The river just here was about 300 feet wide so that from one side we were safe, but further along the track, we could see flames creeping up on three sides ..."

Within 90 minutes Fernie had virtually vanished. That there were any buildings left at all was due to the efforts of volunteer firemen and the freak nature of the wind. The brewery was gone, the first building to be burned. So were Fernie's 11 hotels and everything belonging to the CPR—freight shed, coal chutes, freight and coal cars, two Pullmans, a mile of track, and the depot. Great Northern saved their station and water tank but coal cars in front of the depot were melted.

Every retail house in town was in ashes, as was the new post office, skating rink, four banks, school, two newspaper offices, and the brand new provincial building. In all, over 1,000 buildings were destroyed. Only 23 houses survived, leaving some 6,000 citizens homeless.

The only fortunate aspect of the holocaust was that as far as could be determined, only 10 people died. The *Cranbrook Herald* on August 6, 1908, reported that the dead included "F. Ford, wife and children, of West Fernie, who were found in a well and the condition of the bodies shows they had actually been boiled. Mrs. Turner, of Fernie Annex. Lena Wood, a coloured resident of the restricted district. Four foreigners found in Old Town, names unknown."

In response to the telegraphed plea "City total loss, 6,000 homeless ... need tents," the neighbouring community of Cranbrook had a train on the way in 40 minutes. Spokane, Washington, had another train underway in just over one hour. The Cranbrook train arrived at midnight and exchanged its provisions and clothes for refugees. Every household in Cranbrook took them in, clothed and fed them. Money and supplies poured in from B.C. and elsewhere and citizens of Fernie responded with bravado and courage. An advertisement in the *Free Press* shows their spirit: "When the Smoke Clears Away, You Will Find Us Doing Business at the Old Stand." The paper itself was proof of the aid that poured into the devastated community. It suddenly found itself with a complete new printing plant, sent in unasked for by a Winnipeg firm.

Within a year the city was virtually re-established. A 1910 report listed 3 sawmills, a foundry, a brick factory, a brewery, 15 hotels, 4 cigar stores, a cigar factory, curling and skating rinks, 3 theatres, 3 banks, 7 wholesale houses, 5 churches, 6 lodges, 10 labour unions, and 2 weekly newspapers.

The coal industry was healthy and in 1913 there was a record output at Coal Creek. Some 825,815 tons of coal were moved with 1,478 men employed. Population had risen to 5,000 and the harrowing fire faded into history.

Citizens, however, were still alert. The curse placed by the Indian woman threatened disaster by water as well as by fire. In 1911 there were anxious days when what was described as "the heaviest snowfall in living memory" stranded CPR passenger trains in Fernie. Food was getting scarce when relief trains finally punched through. While the heavy snow didn't cause any known deaths, the potential was always present. In December 1912 a massive rock and snow slide crashed onto Coal Creek mine, demolishing the carpenter and electrical shops and killing six men.

The winter of 1915–16 was another snow year, with over 16 feet falling, in some places covering even the upper windows of houses. In previous years Fernie had often been swept by rampaging floods, forcing residents in low-lying Annex, Annex Extension, and West Fernie to move to higher ground. The worst flood, however, occurred in the spring of 1916. Among other damage, it washed away a bridge and the pipeline from Fairy Creek supplying the city's water. All summer long, water for the town had to be supplied from the Coal Creek reservoir. Sydney Hutcheson recalls in his book, *The Curse*, that a gully ran diagonally across their backyard and there was two feet of water in their house.

During the townspeople's ordeals by floods and fire there had been no further disasters to miners. After the lethal bumps in mines No. 2 and No. 3 a new mine known as No. 1 East was opened in 1911 on the seam above. It became the most important one in the colliery's operation, with a new method of operation that made everyone hope that the problem of bumps had been resolved. Although the potentially deadly bumps still occurred, nearly all gave sufficient warning for workers to escape. One instance was in November 1916. A bump shook the surrounding countryside like an earthquake. It completely destroyed part of No. 1 East but caused no deaths.

Looking like a war zone, Fernie's Victoria Avenue was the scene of utter devastation the morning after the fire. Over 6,000 residents were left homeless.

Unfortunately, an explosion at No. 3 on April 5, 1917, was disastrous. There were 34 men underground. All died. One man was found alive at the foot of the slope but died later, bringing the total to 35. Rescuers found the bodies badly burned and crushed or buried under massive rockfalls, one of which buried the mine locomotive and all 18 cars it had been hauling.

After this disastrous explosion, improvement of the ventilation system, introduction of a gas detector that would pick up lower percentages, electric safety lamps, and spraying and rock-dusting of roadways brought 10 years without any loss of life. During that time probably 200 blowouts had taken place without fatal injuries until August 30, 1928. Shortly before noon on that day an outburst of gas and coal in No. 1 East mine killed six miners.

Seven months later there was trouble again in No. 1 East. On March 25, 1929, indications of fire were noticed coming from a caved roadway in No. 1 East. Operations to remove the heated material started at once but progress was slow for the coal seam had been very thick and the roof had caved badly. It took men almost three weeks to fight their way to the fire. On April 12 a small explosion slightly burned two men. The next day a fall or slide took place above the fire and although everything had been saturated with water, the fall was accompanied by coal dust. It immediately exploded, seriously burning 10 men. Luckily, no lives were lost.

Another 10-year interval of quiet followed the 1928 and 1929 outbursts. Then on September 20, 1938, a violent bump wrecked the main entry to the East slope. Four miners were seriously injured and three killed.

In addition to the series of mine accidents, the community had other difficulties. The early 1920s were marked by labour troubles and strikes, compounded in August 1923 when the Home Bank went broke, owing $800,000. Hundreds of residents lost their life savings.

Then came the Depression of the 1930s with the mines operating only two days a week. Nine out of 10 families were on relief. The 1930s also resulted in another ominous development. Ever since 1904 the Great Northern Railway had provided a second rail line to the coal mines via Rexford, Montana, through Fernie to Michel. In 1926 the GNR abandoned its line between Elko and Michel, using CPR tracks for its daily train. In 1936 the GNR reduced service to a mixed passenger and freight train once a week. Then in 1938 the service was terminated, the rails from Elko to the U.S. border removed. Great Northern's withdrawal was a serious blow to Coal Creek mines for it had been the chief customer for many years.

Although World War Two brought increased demand for coal, when hostilities ended, there was for Fernie a disastrous development. Increasingly, railways replaced with diesel engines the coal-burning locomotives that had sustained the Crowsnest Pass mines. In 1958, despite a newly installed $1.5 million steel tipple, Coal Creek mine was closed. Although it had yielded some 20 million tons of coal and could have kept producing, a changing civilization had relegated steam-powered trains to history books and coal-burning cook stoves and furnaces to museums.

"The closure will kill our city," lamented Fernie's mayor. "The mine employed 400 men. About 30 can find jobs in Michel but the rest will have to leave and then there won't be anyone left to pay the taxes."

The mayor's concern was well founded, since even Michel was fated to disappear in a few years. Then someone remembered the curse invoked by the distraught Indian mother over 60 years previously. Certainly the Crowsnest Pass seemed to be under some type of bad omen. As predicted, residents had suffered "... fire, flood, strife and discord," and over 600 had perished. Perhaps they had now paid the penalty for the alleged wrong done to the Indian maiden so long ago; perhaps now the curse could be lifted.

Accordingly, when Highway 3A was opened in August 1964, Chief Big Crane of the Tobacco Plains Indians arrived from Montana. With him were 40 members of his band, their purpose to lift the curse. They did so with a solemn ritual of song, chant, and the throb of drums. Since then, fate has been kinder to Fernie.

A vast new market for coal developed in Japan, not for steam engines or home heating but for thermal and metallurgical use in steel mills. Demand grew year by year, with production soon surpassing the years from the early 1900s to the late 1940s, when 1 million tons was considered exceptional. By contrast, in 1981 alone Westar Mining shipped over 7 million tons.

Because of this development, Fernie's income rose from just over $15 million in 1971 to nearly $70 million in 1981. Today new schools and a hospital, senior citizens' housing, modern subdivisions, a major ski development amid the spectacular Rocky Mountain scenery, a curling rink, ice arena, and nine-hole golf course enable her citizens to enjoy a blend of the modern and the historical. Much of the downtown area retains its heritage of 1908, when, after the calamitous fire, buildings were rebuilt of brick and stone.

For visitors, Fernie's Tourist Information Centre can provide information on these historic buildings and other local points of interest. One is the burning coal mine at Coal Creek, five miles from Fernie. When the seam caught fire is not known, though old-timers favour about 1916.

Many communities born with Fernie during the early 1900s—Coal Creek, Hosmer, Morrissey, Natal, and Michel—have disappeared. Although Fernie on many occasions seemed fated to follow, she has not only survived but is today one of the largest communities in the Crowsnest Pass.

Within a year the courageous community had rebounded, with substantial new buildings built of stone, concrete, and brick.

THE CROWSNEST PASS
LIVES ON

The Alberta communities of Frank and Hillcrest still survive, although not independently. Today they are part of the Municipality of Crowsnest Pass, formed when the mining communities of Bellevue, Hillcrest, Frank, Blairmore, and Coleman amalgamated in 1979. The municipality has a combined population of some 6,300 and extends for about nine miles along Highway 3. Tourist facilities include shopping malls, campgrounds, motels, underground mine tours, and a museum. In addition, there is the impressive Frank Slide Interpretive Centre and Leitch Collieries Provincial Historic Site, both administered by the Alberta government.

Leitch Collieries Provincial Historic Site is at the Alberta entrance to the pass on Highway 3, west of the small community of Lundbreck. This site, once the location of an 1881 NWMP outpost, was known as Police Flats. Leitch Collieries started operations on Byron Creek in 1907, then expanded across the creek's valley to become one of the largest and most ambitious coal mining projects in the pass. A sophisticated processing plant was established near the old outpost in 1909. Here, company president Malcolm Leitch and mine manager William Hamilton, with big dreams and expectations, built a large sandstone powerhouse, a coal-washing plant that was the tallest building in the pass, and 101 coke ovens. The ovens were built from more than 1 million bricks, all imported from Pennsylvania.

The mining town that sprang up around the Collieries was named Passburg by the mine manager's wife, Mrs. Hamilton, who envisaged it as the main city of the pass. Built on a plain just west of Leitch Collieries, the town included miners' houses, a school, a hotel, and a general store. The adjacent mine manager's sandstone residence was the showpiece of the pass, with running water, electricity, a dumb waiter, and a room for visiting church ministers. Unfortunately, Leitch Collieries, like most coal mine operations in the pass, had a short life.

Top: *Leitch Collieries, circa 1909, consisted of a manager's house, power–house, wash house, and stable.*

Bottom: *The well-preserved stone shell of the powerhouse can still be seen at Leitch Collieries Provincial Historic Site.*

The boom years didn't come soon enough, and the large capital outlay was never recovered. After eight years, the Collieries closed its doors. While Passburg has disappeared except for a few foundations where buildings once stood, the sandstone walls of the mine manager's residence and the mine powerhouse still stand.

They, too, seemed fated to disappear. Fortunately, the Crowsnest Pass Historical Society convinced the Alberta government that the ruins were an important historical asset. As a result, they were designated a provincial historical site. Ruins were stabilized and interpretive panels installed. The sandstone shell of the powerhouse is the main attraction, along with displays graphically portraying life in a typical mining community almost a century ago. The site includes picnic facilities, washrooms, and a large parking area. In summer, daily guided tours are available.

After Leitch Collieries, the next point of interest is the miniature drive-in chapel just off Highway 3 in Bellevue. This tiny chapel is second only to the Frank Slide and the Burmis tree, a haunting 300-year-old rare Limber Pine, as the most photographed attraction in the Crowsnest Pass. Built by Chris Withage of Lethbridge, who donated his labour, it has a seating capacity of eight and features recorded music and sermons.

With a seating capacity of eight, the miniature drive-in chapel at Bellevue features recorded music and sermons.

Bellevue was born in 1901 when nearby coal deposits were discovered. It, too, has known tragedy, the worst in 1910 when 30 men died in a coal-mine explosion. In 1920 more deaths occurred when two policemen were killed in a shootout with two robbers at the Bellevue Café. One of the robbers was killed, the second later captured and hanged. Bellevue today has a population of 1,200 and a variety of visitor services, including a campground with full hookups and the café where the shootout occurred. (A full account of the fatal misadventure is contained in the Heritage House book, *Outlaws and Lawmen of Western Canada, Volume Three.*)

In Bellevue, a glimpse of the region's coal-mining history is offered through a tour of the mine, which operated from 1903 to 1961. A portion of the original tunnel has been opened to visitors, with guided tours from May 15 until Labour Day and pre-booked tours available the rest of the year. To provide a genuine experience of working conditions, the only light comes from miners' lamps issued to visitors. Since the temperature in the mine is about 45°F, visitors should wear warm clothing and sturdy footwear. For current information, phone the Crowsnest Pass Ecomuseum Trust at 403-564-4700 or visit www.bellevuemine.ca.

Across the Crowsnest River from Bellevue on the south side of Highway 3 is the historic community of Hillcrest, with its graveyard containing over 100 of the 189 miners killed in the 1914 explosion. The paved access road is well marked. Hillcrest is now a residential community of 800. One historical point of interest is the building where those killed in the disaster were placed prior to the mass funeral. Hillcrest is also the eastern terminus of the old road through the Frank Slide.

About two miles west of Bellevue is the old town of Frank, with the Frank Slide Interpretive Centre just over a half-mile north of Highway 3. From the Centre, Turtle Mountain dominates the skyline to the southeast, with the slide filling the foreground; to the west are the communities of Blairmore and Coleman, and the landmark of Crowsnest Mountain; eastward lie Bellevue and Hillcrest. At the Centre, interpretive programs, display panels, and award-winning audiovisual presentations, "In The Mountain's Shadow" and "On the Edge of Destruction—the Frank Slide Story," tell not only the story of the Frank Slide, but also the mining and social history of the Crowsnest Pass. In addition, a hiking trail about one mile long through the slide

The Frank Slide Interpretive Centre, near the foot of scarred Turtle Mountain, is a rich repository of Crowsnest Pass history.

gives visitors a personal look at the destruction wreaked by this devastating avalanche of rock. The Centre has picnic sites, a gift shop, and a large parking area. It is open daily from 9:00 a.m. to 6:00 p.m. in summer, and 10:00 a.m. to 5:00 p.m. in winter. For more information, call 403-562-7388 or visit www.frankslide.com.

Like Hillcrest, Frank is largely a residential community of about 200 residents. The site of the original town is now an industrial park, although a fire hydrant and the basement depressions of some of the original buildings from the early 1900s are still visible.

From Frank, a road heads up Gold Creek Valley to the ghost town of Lille, although the four-mile route is rough and a four-wheel drive vehicle is recommended.

Lille was born in 1901 when J.J. Fleutot and C. Remy of the British Columbia Gold Fields Company found promising seams of coal at the base of Grassy Mountain. They opened a mine primarily to supply coal to the Canadian Pacific Railway. The community that grew up around the mine was first named French Camp, then later renamed Lille. By 1907, the population had reached 700, with services that included a hotel, school, and 15-bed hospital. Unfortunately, as miners dug deeper into the mountain the quality of the coal deteriorated and expenses rose. Consequently, the mine closed in 1913. Today the only signs of the community are indentations where buildings once stood, and rows of crumbling coke ovens built of expensive bricks specially imported from Belgium.

Just west of Frank on Highway 3 is Blairmore, born in 1903. With a population of 2,500, it is the largest of the Alberta Crowsnest Pass communities. Its services include a wide variety of businesses, a swimming pool, golf course, museum, liquor store, RCMP headquarters, campground with full hookups, and, for winter visitors, a ski hill, jump, and other facilities.

Top: *The World's Biggest Piggy Bank is one of Coleman's claims to fame.*

Bottom: *The old Coleman High School, a gracious brick building over 50 years old, was given new life by the Crowsnest Historical Society and community volunteers. It now functions as the Crowsnest Museum.*

Adjoining Blairmore to the west on Highway 3 is Coleman. Born in 1904 with the discovery of rich coal deposits in the area, it has a population of 2,000 and a wide variety of businesses. In addition, it claims to possess the world's biggest piggy bank. "Ten Ton Toots," an old compound compressed-air locomotive, is used by the Coleman Lions Club as a fundraiser. A plaque tells us, "This is Ten Ton Toots, known to miners as a 'Dinky.' From 1904 to 1954 Toots hauled five million tons of coal to daylight over 180,000 miles of underground tracks. Toots is a 7 x 7 x 14 compound air locomotive, using compressed air at 800 pounds pressure to pull up to 200-ton loads. Toots invites your inspection and contribution."

Another attraction in Coleman is the Crowsnest Museum, a credit to the Crowsnest Historical Society. As the Society notes: "Our general purpose is to collect, preserve, and portray the heritage of the

Crowsnest Pass and district through natural history specimens, artifacts, documents, maps, pictures, and information which is significant to the history of the area."

The museum is located in the former Coleman High School, a gracious brick building now over 50 years old. The Society purchased the building for $1 and with volunteer help turned it into a museum that represents the Alberta section of the Crowsnest Pass. The project is ongoing, but completed displays include a room depicting a typical early commercial centre complete with dentist's office, blacksmith's shop, general store, and barbershop.

Another room depicts community life and includes a pioneer school and a miner's cottage. A naval exhibit commemorates HMCS *Blairmore*, a minesweeper that formed part of the Royal Canadian Navy during the Second World War. Upstairs, a fish-and-wildlife diorama depicts the region's wildlife heritage, from streams to forests to alpine country.

The most recent addition to the museum is the Mining Gallery, which takes you through a portal into the everyday working life of an underground coal miner. It includes such features as time keepers, the lamp house, mine rescue, room and pillar systems, coke ovens, equipment, and the men and horses who worked the mines. The Gallery offers something for everyone, from images and photographs to anecdotal stories. There are several models and individual displays, and you can even have your picture taken in a realistic wash house setting.

Outside on the former school grounds is a large display of mining equipment, including a rail-bending kiln from Greenhill mine and a model of a horse-drawn coal car. There is also a park and rest area. The museum is open year-round, and includes a gift shop (403-563-5434).

At Coleman, a prominent landmark is 9,138-foot Crowsnest Mountain. Coleman is the southern terminus of Kananaskis Highway 940, also known as the Forestry Trunk Road. From Coleman the Kananaskis (Can-an-as-kiss) heads northward 140 miles through the east slopes of the Rocky Mountains to the Trans-Canada Highway at Seebe, 55 miles west of Calgary. Many people consider it to be Alberta's most scenic drive. Half the route is paved, the rest gravel, which is treated to control dust.

The highway cleaves some of Canada's most spectacular mountain scenery and has three summits, each over a mile high. The most

The Crowsnest Pass, one of Canada's most spectacular regions, can be nurturing or dangerous. This old timer takes it all in stride.

impressive is Highwood Pass, 90 miles north of Coleman. At 7,238 feet it is the highest piece of engineered road in Canada. Snow usually stays until the end of June and can return in late September. Even in mid-summer, patches lie in the shade of stunted larch and pine. Another impressive piece of geography is "the Gap." Here the Oldman River flows through what seems a solid wall of rock—the Livingstone Range. A noticeable feature is that the mountains along the route are different from those flanking other thoroughfares in the Rockies. Some are grey, some are red, while some have whorls resembling gigantic fingerprints over 1,000 feet high. Still others are criss-crossed by massive crevices, vivid evidence of the cataclysmic upheaval that led to the birth of the Rocky Mountains 60-70 million years ago.

The treasure of the route is Kananaskis Provincial Park. Here the Alberta government has spent millions of dollars to create a magnificent outdoor playground amidst some 90 square miles of glaciers, lakes, streams, and mountain meadows. There are hundreds of campsites with fireplaces, boat-launching facilities, and hiking trails. The region is also popular in winter, with a variety of cross-country ski trails, ice-fishing, and snowboarding. Kananaskis Village Resort provides world-class facilities and is open all year.

For the Alberta section of the Crowsnest Pass, an era ended in 1983 when the last coal mine closed. This mine, operated by Coleman Collieries Limited, employed 725 men at

The Terex Titan, the largest tandem-axle dump truck in the world and the only one of its kind, dwarfs a standard pickup truck. It can be viewed during mine tours.

its peak in 1976. But decreasing demand led to a steady reduction in the work force, until only 80 employees were left. When they were laid off, an industry that had endured for over 80 years became history.

By contrast, while mining in the Alberta section of the pass was declining, the B.C. part was booming. Since 1980, for instance, over $1 billion has been invested in coal mines. This investment has dramatically changed coal mining, the coal miners, and the communities. The revolution began in 1947 in the Natal–Michel area, when Crowsnest Industries began strip mining for coal. With this system there are no underground tunnels. The overburden is stripped off the coal seams, and the coal is extracted with massive machines and hauled away by equally massive 240-ton trucks.

While the 240-ton trucks are huge, they are dwarfed by one vehicle called the Terex Titan. It has a 3,300-horsepower locomotive engine, and rear wheels powered by electric motors that could supply 3,200 homes with electricity. Its box can hold two Greyhound buses and two pickups, and it weighs 1 million pounds fully loaded. In addition to being the largest tandem-axle dump truck in the world and the only one of its kind, the Titan had an appetite to match its name, since it used up to 550 gallons of diesel fuel every eight hours. After several years, however, it was retired because of the cost of upkeep. It can still be viewed during tours of the mine.

But while the Titan and its 1-million-pound capacity is impressive, so is the size of the coalfield. One firm alone estimates its reserves at 7 billion tons. The technology used today in extracting this coal has transformed the traditional picks and shovels into museum pieces.

The Elkview mine, located in the Elk Valley region of southeastern British Columbia just over three miles from Sparwood, is one of Canada's largest open pit mines. Its active mining area measures approximately seven miles by three miles and has more than 50 miles of roads around it. The coal is covered with shale, sandstone, and overburden ranging from a few feet to upwards of 1,000. For every ton of coal mined, up to 13 tons of this waste rock must be removed. To do so, the modern miner drills blast patterns consisting of around 250 holes measuring more than 50 feet in depth. These patterns are then loaded with over 330,000 pounds of explosives. When detonated, the explosives loosen and fragment the waste rock, which is then hauled away, leaving the coal behind. Bulldozers then break up the coal, which is in seams of between 5 and 50 feet thick. The large shovels then load haul trucks that transport the broken coal to a conveyor. The conveyor carries the coal to the central breaker system, where it is crushed, then transported through a one-and-a-half-mile tunnel by another conveyor to the raw coal silos.

However, the coal is not yet ready to be used as coke in steel mills around the world. First it must be washed to obtain the specific qualities required by the mine's customers. During the washing process, coal is conveyed from the raw coal silos to a preparation plant visible from the town of Sparwood, where it is screened to remove debris. Coal larger than one centimetre in diameter is washed in heavy-media vessels and delivered directly to the clean coal silos. Finer coal is screened in two sizes for washing by a separate process. After washing, the two size fractions are recombined and conveyed to a thermal dryer to reduce the moisture content. Once the coal is dried it is conveyed to one of four clean coal silos to await loading onto unit trains.

At the rail load-out area, computerized measuring equipment ensures that each car is loaded to its capacity of approximately 100 tons.

At the same time, a latex emulsion is sprayed over each full carload to prevent dust from escaping during the more than 600-mile trip west to ports in Vancouver.

The unit trains, operated by Canadian Pacific, were built especially for carrying coal. Each hauls about 11,000 metric tons and is over a mile long. The coal is loaded into the train as it pulls through Elkview's rail loop at about one-third of a mile per hour. Each unit train has on average 111 cars and takes about 4 hours to load. Once the train has completed loading, it starts a three-day journey to ports in Vancouver. When the trains arrive at either of the two ports—Neptune or Westshore Terminals—the trains are unloaded into stockpiles of various products. It is from these stockpiles that the ships transporting Elkview's coal to the world are loaded.

Visitors interested in seeing an open-pit mine can do so in July and August when Elkview conducts tours of its five-mile-long open pit and Terex Titan truck. For tour information and reservations, check with the Sparwood Chamber of Commerce Information Centre at 250-425-2423. (In the off-season, group tours for 20 or more people are available.)

The massive development of the coalfields has created new communities and resulted in two of the originals vanishing. These were Natal and Michel, bulldozed and burned, their residents moving to Sparwood a few miles west. Sparwood, designed to provide a pleasing lifestyle in contrast to the drabness of Natal and Michel, has grown into a community of 4,000. It offers a variety of visitor services

Modelled on the late Stanley Wasiewicz, a pick-and-shovel miner for over 70 years, this wooden statue carved with a chainsaw pays tribute to all the region's miners.

and has an excellent Chamber of Commerce Information Centre just off Highway 3. Outside the Centre is an impressive wooden statue of a miner, which was carved with a chainsaw. Modelled on the late Stanley Wasiewicz, who was a pick- and-shovel miner for over 70 years, it commemorates all of the region's miners. In addition, murals depicting the bygone era of mining are painted on the buildings in downtown Sparwood.

Twenty miles north of Sparwood is Elkford, another community born of coal development. Situated in the Rocky Mountains at the highest elevation for a community in Canada (4,265 feet), Elkford has dubbed itself the "Wilderness Capital of British Columbia." It has a population of 2,600 and visitor services that include accommodation and a municipal campground with 70 sites, as well as showers, washrooms, firepits, and a sani-station. It is the business centre for a huge mining operation by Fording Coal.

In addition to the coal-mine tour, visitors will find other attractions, from fishing and camping to golfing and admiring the Rocky Mountain scenery. Visitors are served by a wide range of businesses, including deluxe motels, government-run campgrounds, modern ski facilities, and shopping centres.

The Crowsnest Pass in Alberta–B.C. has been buffeted harshly by fate in the past. Those days are history, and the region today is optimistic and prosperous. While coal remains king, visitors will find the welcome mat out at all communities along this 60-mile-long ribbon of pavement through the Rocky Mountains.

CHAPTER NOTES

Preface

[1] http://www.cybercloud.com/turtle/synopsis.html

Pass of Triumph, Pass of Tragedy

[2] Ratch, "An Impossible Curse: The Ghostrider on Hosmer Mountain," in *The Forgotten Side of the Border: British Columbia's Elk Valley and Crowsnest Pass*, p. 3.

[3] Cousins, *A History of the Crow's Nest Pass*, p. 20.

[4] Ibid., p. 21.

[5] http://www.sparwood.bc.ca/virtualmuseum/18_05mphillipps.html

[6] Ratch, "An Impossible Curse," p. 8.

[7] Ibid., pp. 7-8.

[8] Smyth, *Tales of the Kootenays*, p. 68.

[9] Ratch, "An Impossible Curse," p. 8.

[10] Mouat, "James Baker and William Fernie: The Politics of Development in the Crowsnest Coalfields," in *The Forgotten Side of the Border: British Columbia's Elk Valley and Crowsnest Pass*, p. 16.

[11] Ibid.

Railroad Through the Crowsnest

[12] Miller, *Fort Steele: Gold Rush to Boom Town*, p. 46.

[13] Mouat, "James Baker and William Fernie," p. 18.

[14] Ibid.

[15] Ibid., p. 19.

[16] Ibid.

[17] http://www.fernie.com/about_fernie/rail_wars.html

[18] Eagle, *The Canadian Pacific Railway and the Development of Western Canada*, p. 31.

[19] Ibid., p. 17.

[20] Mouat, "James Baker and William Fernie," p. 22.

[21] Ibid., p. 23.

[22] Dawson, *Crowsnest: An Illustrated History and Guide to The Crowsnest Pass*, p. 18.

[23] Eagle, *The Canadian Pacific*, p. 57.

[24] Ibid.

[25] Ibid.

[26] Ibid., p. 58.

[27] Rodney, *Kootenai Brown: Canada's Unknown Frontiersman*, p. 177.

[28] Eagle, *The Canadian Pacific*, p. 59.

[29] Ibid.

[30] Rodney, *Kootenai Brown*, p. 178.

[31] Eagle, *The Canadian Pacific*, p. 59.

[32] http://www.crowsnest.bc.ca/construction05.html

[33] Stuart, *Some We Have Met and Stories They Have Told*, p. 14.

[34] Eagle, *The Canadian Pacific*, p. 59.

[35] Ibid., p. 60.

[36] Ibid.

[37] Ibid.

[38] Ibid., p. 53.

BIBLIOGRAPHY

Books

Cousins, William James. *A History of the Crow's Nest Pass*. Edmonton, AB: Historic Trails Society of Alberta, 1981.

Dawson, Brian J. *Crowsnest: An Illustrated History and Guide to The Crowsnest Pass*. Vancouver, BC: Altitude Publishing Canada, Ltd., 1995.

Dempsey, Hugh A., ed. *The CPR West: The Iron Road and the Making of a Nation*. Vancouver, BC: Douglas & McIntyre, 1984.

Downs, Art, ed. *Pioneer Days in British Columbia, volume two*. Surrey, BC: Heritage House Publishing Company Ltd., 1975-1979.

———. *Pioneer Days in British Columbia, volume four*. Surrey, BC: Heritage House Publishing Company Ltd., 1979.

Eagle, John A. *The Canadian Pacific Railway and the Development of Western Canada*. Kingston, ON: McGill-Queen's University Press, 1989.

Harvey, R.G. *Carving the Western Path By River, Rail, and Road Through B.C.'s Southern Mountains*. Surrey, BC: Heritage House Publishing Company Ltd., 1998.

———. *Carving the Western Path By River, Rail, and Road Through Central and Northern B.C.* Surrey, BC: Heritage House Publishing Company Ltd., 1999.

————. "The Crows Nest Railway." *British Columbia Historical News: Journal of the British Columbia Historical Federation, vol. 37, no. 3, summer 2004.* Victoria: British Columbia Historical Federation, 2004.

Hungry Wolf, Adolf. *Rails in the Canadian Rockies.* Skookumchuck, BC: Canadian Caboose Press, 1993.

Miller, Naomi. *Fort Steele: Gold Rush to Boom Town.* Surrey, BC: Heritage House Publishing Company Ltd., 2002.

Miller, Naomi and Norton, Wayne, eds. *The Forgotten Side of the Border: British Columbia's Elk Valley and Crowsnest Pass.* Kamloops, BC: Plateau Press, 1998.

Mouat, Jeremy. "James Baker and William Fernie: The Politics of Development in the Crowsnest Coalfields," in *The Forgotten Side of the Border: British Columbia's Elk Valley and Crowsnest Pass.* Miller, Naomi and Norton, Wayne, eds. Kamloops, BC: Plateau Press, 1998.

Ratch, Noel. "An Impossible Curse: The Ghostrider on Hosmer Mountain," in *The Forgotten Side of the Border: British Columbia's Elk Valley and Crowsnest Pass.* Miller, Naomi and Norton, Wayne, eds. Kamloops, BC: Plateau Press, 1998.

Rodney, William. *Kootenai Brown: Canada's Unknown Frontiersman.* Surrey, BC: Heritage House Publishing Company Ltd., 1996.

Ross, Jane and Tracy, William. *Hiking the Historic Crowsnest Pass.* Calgary, AB: Rocky Mountain Books, 2001.

Scullion, Bob and Thirkell, Fred. *British Columbia 100 Years Ago: Portraits of a Province.* Surrey, BC: Heritage House Publishing Company Ltd., 2002.

Silversides, Brock V. *Waiting for the Light: Early Mountain Photography in British Columbia & Alberta, 1865-1939.* Saskatoon, SK: Fifth House Publishers, 1995.

Smyth, Fred J. *Tales of the Kootenays.* Vancouver, BC: Douglas & McIntyre, 1997.

Stuart, Will. *Some We Have Met and Stories They Have Told.* Creston, BC: The Creston Review Ltd., 1958.

Turnbull, Elsie G. *Ghost Towns and Drowned Towns of West Kootenay.* Surrey, BC: Heritage House Publishing Company Ltd., 1988.

Websites

http://www.crowsnest.bc.ca/construction.html
http://www.crowsnest-highway.ca/

http://www.cybercloud.com/turtle/synopsis.html
http://www.fernie.com/about_fernie/rail_wars.html
http://www.frankslide.com/faq.html
http://www.sparwood.bc.ca/virtualmuseum/18_05mphillipps.html
http://members.tripod.com/~coalminersmemorial/
http://www.teckcominco.com/operations/coalpartnership/
partnership.htm

PHOTO CREDITS

Front cover: aerial image of Turtle Mountain and the Frank Slide, showing the Flathead range beyond, courtesy of the Frank Slide Interpretive Centre, Alberta Community Development; inset of coal miners at Hillcrest, Provincial Archives of Alberta (A-2415)

Back cover, top: Fernie fire, Heritage House collection; bottom left: rescue team for the Hillcrest mine disaster, Provincial Archives of Alberta (A-2413); bottom right: trestle on Crow's Nest Pass Railway, Glenbow Archives (ND-9-37)

B.C. Archives: pp. 15 (A-01071)

Glenbow Archives: pp. 19 (NA-936-37), 31 top (NA-943-45), 31 bottom (ND-9-37), 34-35 (NA-3903-82), 37 (NA-5656-11), 43 (NA-3658-100), 44-45 (NA-1494-11), 47 top (NA-919-34), 47 bottom (NA-659-76), 49 (ND-9-20), 50 (ND-9-18), 51 (ND-9-36)

National Film Board: pp. 8 top (81768)

Fort Steele Archives: pp. 13 left (F.S. 5-62)

Heritage House Collection: pp. 8 bottom inset, 13 left, 21, 24 top, 24 bottom, 27, 30, 39, 59, 70-71, 72, 74, 75, 76, 79, 80, 81, 82-83, 87, 88-89, 94-95, 100, 104, 114, 123, 124, 127, 130, 131 left, 131 right, 134, 135, 139, 141, 143, 146-147, 150, 152 top, 152 bottom, 153, 155, 156 top, 156 bottom, 158, 159, 161

Provincial Archives of Alberta: pp. 5 (A-2419), 10-11 (A-2414), 54-55 (B-2452), 102 (A-2415), 106-107 (A-1784), 118 (A-2413), 122 (A-1778), 128-129 (A-2411)

Silverton Historical Society: pp. 32

Vern Decoux: pp. 16

MAP CREDITS

University of Victoria library map collection: pp. 28
Heritage House collection: pp. 8 bottom, 68, 111

Photographs and maps included in this book have been donated or purchased from a variety of sources and are reprinted based on conditions of use at the time of purchase.

INDEX